More Praise for *Creative Intimacy*

"Dr. Laurie Moore knows how to access positive solutions
in her own life and makes it easy for the rest of us to do the
same. *Creative Intimacy* is a convenient road map for those
who desire more harmony in their relationships."

—Jacquelyn Aldana, author of *The Fifteen Minute Miracle Revealed* and *The Miracle Manifestation Manual*

"All I can say is wow! Dr. Laurie Moore's perspective contributed to my marriage in ways I didn't expect! Dr. Laurie Moore is
uniquely talented."

—Marvin Cohen, President and co-founder of LifePartnerQuest, Relationship Coach,
father, and husband

Creative Intimacy

A Practical Guide to Better Relationships

Creative
Intimacy

A Practical Guide to Better Relationships

Laurie Moore, PhD

 Frog, Ltd.
Berkeley, California

Published by Frog, Ltd.
Frog, Ltd. Books are distributed by
North Atlantic Books, P O Box 12327, Berkeley, California 94712

Cover and book design © 2001 Carolina de Bartolo.
Editors: Bob Giges, Kathy Glass, Nancy Kirwan.

North Atlantic Books are available through most bookstores. For further information, call 800-337-2665 or visit our website at www.northatlantic-books.com. Substantial discounts on bulk quantities are available to corporations, professional associations, and other organizations. For details and discount information, contact our special sales department.

Library of Congress Cataloging-in-Publication Data
Moore, Laurie.
     Creative intimacy : a practical guide to better relationships / by Laurie Moore.
          p. cm.
     ISBN 1-58394-019-7 (alk. paper)
          1. Man-woman relationships. 2. Creative ability.
3. Interpersonal relations. 4. Intimacy (Psychology) I. Title
HQ801 .M66 2001
306.7--dc21   2001033341

     1   2   3   4   5   6   7   8   9 / 04   03   02   01

Table of Contents

Foreword   xi

Acknowledgements   xiii

Introduction   1
My Personal Experience with Creative Intimacy

1 • Creative Personality Types   9
Each Personality Type's Way of Living

2 • Creative Romance   27
Improving Sex With Your New Perspectives

3 • Creative Communication   47
Growing Closer and Happier When Conflict Arises

4 • Creative Self-Care   57
Becoming the Source of Your Own Happiness

5 • Creative Empowerment   67
Knowing Your Life Purpose

6 · **Creative Support**   75
Clarifying and Communicating What You Need

7 · **Creative Spirituality**   93
How You Speak With Life

8 · **Creative Decision-Making**   117
Involving Different Parts of Your Personality in a Decision

9 · **Creative Projects**   133
Alternatives to Ongoing Conflict With
the Help of Artistic Media

10 · **Creative Intimacy**   155
Making the Most of Relationship Opportunities

Products Created by Dr. Laurie Moore   163
Ordering Information

Foreword • by Carolyn Godschild Miller

Choosing a book on relationship is like trying to pick just one piece of chocolate from a tempting assortment. What you hope for is the literary equivalent of a delectable cherry, nut, or caramel. What you get is often a big disappointment. *Creative Intimacy*, however, is one guide to love you'll devour with gusto! It's a thoroughly delicious read, and it packs the kind of intellectual and emotional nutrition a growing mind requires.

Dr. Laurie Moore serves up an ingenious model for healing relationships by identifying what it is that we, and our romantic partners, truly need and want from each other. She describes twelve distinct Creative Personality Types, each of which relates to the world in a different way, and helps us identify our personal creative style, and that of our partner. She then shows how thorny interpersonal conflicts can often be quickly resolved when lovers call upon little-used aspects of their personalities to better meet each others' needs and expectations.

I especially like the way *Creative Intimacy* keeps the focus on self-knowledge, rather than self-improvement. Recognizing that if we knew better, we would do better, Moore provides a wealth of exercises designed to help us identify our true feelings and desires, and bring creative solutions into sharp focus. The process is brought to life by the intriguing stories of couples and individuals who tried her unique approach to conflict resolution and found that it worked!

Dr. Laurie Moore makes a very compelling case for the idea that self-awareness, gratitude, and mutual understanding can often resurrect the joyful intimacy in relationships that seemed destined for the scrap heap. If you are tired of simply giving up whenever a promising love affair bogs down in apparently irreconcilable differences, this book is for you. If you are willing to examine your own contribution to a painful romantic stalemate, but don't know how, this book is for you. If you deeply believe that love is meant to be easy, spontaneous, and fun but have never experienced it that way, this book is definitely for you.

■ ■ ■

Carolyn Godschild Miller, Ph.D., is the author of *Soulmates: Following Inner Guidance to the Relationship of Your Dreams,* and *Creating Miracles: Understanding the Experience of Divine Intervention.*

Acknowledgements

I would like to acknowledge people who have contributed to this book either by helping directly or with their encouragement, friendship, and ongoing support.

Thank you Ray Torres. Your effulgent love fills me with goodness and happiness. You are a precious soul, a sunray of light, a moon ray of love, and a blessing in my life. I thank you with deep fondness, respect, honor, and all the love of my heart and soul.

Thank you Mark Mlawer. Your generous care has deeply touched and strengthened me. You are forever dear to my heart.

Thank you Jessie-boy, sweet loving Buddha cat. You sit with me while I meditate and write bringing me joy and peace each day.

Thank you Maria Marcusson, brave warrior sister of many years, wise, intelligent and loving friend. You make my life rich.

Thank you adorable Lisa Levinson, my courageous and insightful sister of many years, kind and caring friend. You bring me delight.

Thank you to friends who bring love and light to me year after year: Shamaya and Chayim Barton, Gary Hillman, Jim and Barbara Frandeen, David Wicker, Miguel and Peri Santa Cruz. You are family to me.

Thank you to wise, special, and fun friends who have been consistently present for years: Jon Lee and Sara Baker (my guardian angels), Summer Rolphe (my favorite advisor), Karl Schaffer (you bring me great joy by making me laugh and laugh), and Cass Redmon (my very wise friend), and Ruah Bull.

Thank you to wonderful new friends of the past few years and old friends rarely seen but always remembered: Loic Jassy (for your editorial advice as well as your profound inspiration and magical presence), Bobby Giges (for your editorial assistance as well as your generosity, kindness, and care), Lee Ballen, Kai Seidenburg (for your sincerity and deep care), Janette Archer (for your generosity with my business as well as your friendship), Joyce Anue, Marigold Fine, John McCowen, Caitlin Johnson, Alicia Cayuela, Glen Brooks, Catherine Benedict, Lavender, Sharon Kane, Phil Heller (for your support and authenticity), Marvin Cohen, Narrey Caldwell, Rayna Lumbard, Leslie French, Chris Payne, Wayne Landers, Ron Meadow, Elliot Coleman, Bonnie Johansen, Donald Foreman, Darriel Arnott, Kelly Rose, Sonja Shahan, Nicola Geiger, Manne Boise, Haven Thomas, Arbor, Joan Tanheimer, Lee Hemmingway, Ed Demory, Will Cameau, Jay Cloudwalker, Tom Begich, and Marlene and Lenny Sussman.

Thank you Dr. Marty Galvin, who inspired and taught me to write; Brook Moore, who encouraged me to write books; Richard

Fein, a healer who changed my life; Steve Gold, my outstanding business partner; Richard Grossinger, who offered excellent assistance and support; Jennifer Privateer; Mark Robbins, who helped launch the seminars; Shana Ross and Madelyn Keller, who promoted my work; Danny Alaura, who inspired me; Gabrielle Laney, my first graphic artist; David Stein, my multi-talented designer; Al Segal, my workshop assistant; Tany Soussana, my outstanding publicist; Angela Heath, who encouraged me to get this book published, and Mary Embree.

Thank you to my outstanding teachers along the way: Ammachi, Rainya Dann, Rita Kosofksy, Susan Beeler, Sue Grimm, Lindsay Towsend, Linda Klein, Kay Frances Schepp, Bob and Carolyn Doughton, Robert Kaplan, Baba Hari Dass, GuruMai Chidvilasananda, Sai Baba, Terri Halprin-Eaton, Beth Pettingil, Linda and Charlie Bloom, JE Rash, Laura Pfiaff-Pfiefer, David Zimmerman, Walter Bartman, Kali Ray and the Tri-Yoga staff, Elisa Lodge, the magical Jacquelyn Aldana, Gina Palmer, and Mary Margret Rose.

Thank you to Emandal Farm: Emandal Golden Petals Co., Tam and Clive Adams, Riley O'Neil, Miriam Labes and Russell Brown.

Thank you to all of my wonderful clients. You amaze me.

Thank you with all my heart to Mom, Dad, Kenny and Leslie Moore. My family of birth was the nest for all later opportunities I have had to serve and create. I am deeply grateful to have spent my childhood with each of you. You've loved me well.

Thank you to my relatives and their families: Hurwitzes, Edlins, Dwyers, Bermans, Moores, Ginny Robertson, Mary Anne Larson, and my grandparents. Special thanks to cousin

Andrew Berman, Nina Moore, cousin Noel Edlin, Aunt Dorie Edlin, and Uncle Brook Moore for your care and encouragement.

Thank you to special people who encouraged me: Bob Gower, Karen Lintott, Tanya Greenstein, Mark Beaudry, Bari Roberts, Bruce Bratton, Michelle Hayward, David Theirman, Jen Corrina, Connie Finch, Leslyn McCallum, Bob Sleeth, Marla Lipshultz, Gabrielle Russo, Bonnie Park, Willow Simmons, Henry Seltzer, Sheila Gold, Jule Herman, The Ackleys, Charlie Kirshner, Juliette Goetze, Helayne Ballaban, Jay Gleason, Jen Bame, Tanya Greenstein, Paul Suni, Robert Ward, Josi Riley, Susan Matthews Scott, Eric Reed, Shoshana McKnight, Wendy Beallor, Mark Taylor, Skip, Ralph Peduto, Lola Britton, Mark Borax, Sam Burnell, Duke Houston, Nancy Collins, Wendy Wagner, and Geoffa Soukkup.

Thank you to my always-remembered camp sisters: Cindy Amiten, Kerry Gelb, Sara Zimmerman, Curry Rose Mills, Pata Calvo, Lili Aguilar, Cheryl Rice, Lebbie Dewis, Julie Lapides, Emmy Goldstein, Judy Gibbs, Nancy Zussman, Vicky White, Sari Friedlander, and Lisa Melmed.

Thank you to my childhood friends who greatly supported my creativity and service work: Jerry and Jamie MacDougall, Stef and Julie Procopiow, Jennifer and Kitty Sherwin, Debbie and Joanne Lewis, Margret and Barbara Schnipper, Dena Dryer, and Tina Pease.

Thank you to the wonderful people who turned my writing into theater productions: Lisa Kalmanesh, Yolanda Stabler, Francescas Botta, Chris Woldemar, Ben Monmoneir, Bo Bixler,

Shawn Audell, Andrew Shahan, Victoria Stone, Lynn McGurrin, Brigid Ryan, Sandra Blanchard, Sandra Castro and the children at Emandal.

Thank you to my friends' children who are precious and inspiring to me: Yakov Barton, Jorel Jassy, Malika Santa Cruz, Blaire Frandeen, Onowa Tanheimer, and Rowie Santa Cruz.Thank you to the many people who have inspired me whose names are too numerous to mention.

My knowledge is possible because of those who paved the road I travelled: Carl Rodgers, Gay and Kathlyn Hendricks, Natalie Goldberg, Julia Cameron, Caroline Myss, Deepak Chopra, and Carolyn Godschild Miller.

Introduction

My Personal Experience with Creative Intimacy

When I was a girl, I went to a sleep-away camp in the Pocono Mountains of Pennsylvania every summer. Tucked away in the forest, far from the tangled and muffled, argumentative voice of the city, and close to the smell of fresh earth, I was full of my own love. Each day was a celebration of life's preciousness. I went to dance rehearsal and experienced my body whirling as a prayer of love for life.

I loved camp because we slept in cabins with open windows. Nighttime nourished me as I shared the rhythm of breathing with six other girls. That air journeyed in circles, befriending the sweet lake, challenging the forest branches' mysterious guardedness, and dancing through my lungs as I softened into sleep.

Sometimes a counselor would hug me good night, and I could feel like a baby for a moment, fed with the mothering skin and muscle of a body that was bigger and stronger than mine. All summer I lived with these sisters who played and talked with me. This filled a secret guilty longing because I was the oldest child in my family, and my role centered on teaching, surprising, and helping my sister who had multiple disabilities, and my brother who was years younger than I. Although I delighted in loving them, I resented my younger sister and brother who couldn't give me a hand when I was in need. At summer camp, I was an equal and others gave to me.

The cabin was full of autographs from girls who had lived in it as far back as the forties, and this was astounding to me. I felt I related to these girls I had never met because we all knew the secret of life lived in the voice that lit campfires in our hearts. Spirit's voice lived in ours when we sang around the campfire circle. The heart alone was important. Stories that no mind can tell grew, gardened in the muscular earth. We swam in a lake and danced in a wooden playhouse. At night we played capture the flag in the forest. My heart took flight and my mind was at rest.

In the cabin of peers my own age, I was fun, entertaining, and happy. I felt free to be myself with no caution or restraint. In this mode, I was my most authentic self.

Outside of the safe little cabin, however, I was shy. I liked the girls who were older than me but felt nervous in their presence. My taciturn nature in the larger community did not feel like a choice. It got worse each summer, and by the time I was a teenager, it took over me like acne. It oozed and pussed and I hated it. My stomach felt queasy, and my throat tightened when I was out in the larger community. Life was getting more and more challenging.

One spring when I began to daydream about returning to camp, I felt very frustrated. I wanted to be part of the entire camp community. I wanted to share my love and joy with everyone. I longed to do this, but feared I couldn't. My shyness ran my life. As the days brought me closer and closer to camp, I became more and more agitated about the idea of experiencing another timid summer.

Walking by the little creek on my way from school to my house one afternoon, I stopped and listened to the chiming song of water passing over stones. I began to imagine that I was a different person, a gregarious teenager who could be generous with my love. Suddenly, it dawned on me that there was no pre-written script for the summer of 1978. If I wanted to be the life of the party and shine my love on others, I could.

When I got to camp, I spent time visiting every single one of the fifteen cabins to introduce myself, see how the old campers were, and help the new campers to feel at home. I introduced myself to each of the counselors. I felt heart-warmed by my new self-assigned position. I greatly enjoyed the contact and felt deep respect for the many people I was befriending. A simple switch of behavior changed the way that I felt about the cast of characters in my own life.

After the first week of camp, we had an election and someone nominated me to be camp president. Along with five other nominees, I left the campfire circle so that the other girls could vote in privacy. When we returned, I was told that I had won.

I knew that previous camp presidents had been like homecoming queens, crowned with a title for popularity, but I knew that would not be enough for me. The call to become part of community was a call of love, and I wanted to put that love into action. I felt that the camp president had a duty to serve, and I decided that my camp council would make the most of our responsibility and opportunities. We organized creative events, made curtains for all of the cabins, set up our own clubhouse, and did our best to make sure that everyone's friendship, fun, and food needs were attended to.

Counselors were shocked that last year's little shy girl from cabin 12 had become a camp leader. The kids made a plaque that said I was the best president of Camp Netimus ever, and counselors made a wooden gavel engraved with "The best moments of a person's life: their little, unremembered acts of kindness and love."

Guess who was most amazed? I was, because I was being rewarded for being my full self. The river of love ran through my veins. I felt Spirit's grace in my own actions and I overflowed with gratitude because life was offering me such joy. By simply choosing to be more of myself, I lived in delight and awe for all of the amazing people around me. What more could anyone ever want?

My story did not end there because my life continued to present me with numerous occasions to overcome shyness in a variety of other arenas and creatively replace it with love. As a young adult, a performer, a professional, and a lover, I went through more shyness battles. Each triumph brought me deeper into gratitude for life. As a result of changing my roles in problematic situations, I have experienced profound love, ecstatic sex, blissful physical existence, a superb career, outstanding friends, financial rewards, miraculous experiences of union with Spirit, and ongoing gratitude.

My fascination with human expression and change led me to become a theater director in my twenties. I co-wrote, directed, and performed on stage for six years. Actors frequently brought their troubles to me, and I designed drama exercises that allowed them to take on new roles both at rehearsal and in real life. People reported unbelievable yet true life changes as a result, so I decided to go back to school and study psychotherapy. After working with individuals and couples as a counselor for six years, I designed the Creative Intimacy workshop so that people could change their lives in valuable ways.

During my years as a theater director and psychotherapist, I was challenged with many relationship difficulties. I approached each problem I encountered in the same way that I approached my childhood problem with the camp community. I found that I could change every problem by changing my role in the script that I was co-writing and co-directing.

Now I bring my focus to you. How you bring the lesson of my story into your own life is what is most important. This book aims to help you develop an approach to living that will allow you to create a better situation in any area of your life in which you desire more than you are getting.

When you learn to shift your role in the realm of love and relationship to others, you have a key for switching your role in any area of life: friendship, sex, health, money, spirituality, and career. This book focuses on a relationship with a significant other, but it teaches a skill that can be applied to your relationship with anyone and anything, including your boss, your sister, your bank account, yourself, your body, and Spirit. Feel free to apply the techniques to any part of your life in which a change is desired.

You, like most people, probably have an area in your life in which your dream and actual experience are far apart. We live in a time during which people desire perfect compatibility but encounter numerous disappointments. Does your communication with your mate deeply satisfy you, or are you desiring something and not getting it? Are you feeling torn between staying and leaving a relationship? Do you have an ongoing conflict with your significant other that never changes? Are you satisfied with your life in general, or is something missing? Do you want deeper spirituality in your partnership? Could romance and sex be a lot better? Has the flame lessened and a wonderful relationship lost its excitement? Are you hiding things from your partner and feeling lonely because of it? Are you tired of being anxious or depressed over your relationship? Do you feel unsupported, unappreciated, or misunderstood? Do you want to reach your highest potential and be happy? If you answered yes to any of these questions you are ripe for a big, juicy breakthrough.

If you are like me, you have spent sufficient time and money trying to change your problems. Through my experience as a theater director, psychotherapist, and eighteen years in the arts and social services, I have discovered that you can make big turnarounds in your life by accessing new parts of yourself. You, too, have parts of yourself that are hungry to come out and play.

Like actors waiting for the opportunities to audition, your undeveloped characteristics wait on the sidelines for a lucky call from an agent. They need not wait any longer. You are a co-director in your life play, and life is your agent. Life provides endless opportunities for joy and success twenty-four hours a day. What happens is affected by grace and all participants involved, but how you experience and respond to life is chosen by you. When you choose a role that serves your deepest dreams, you prosper, as do those around you.

You have the ability to respond to old problems with entirely new solutions, and this book shows you how in simple and easy ways. Do not let life pass you by. When you remember how to give fully of yourself, both desired and unexpected rewards are abundant. When you creatively interact with situations that challenge you, life is full of pleasure, power, fulfillment, and extraordinary results every single day.

This book cannot take your hand and carry you out of your dissatisfactions, but it can offer you the tools to carry yourself. Birds carry the weight of their own muscles and bones by resting their wings in the lap of the sky. Gracefully spread and rest your most positive thoughts in the arms of life's grace. So much is possible here on Earth.

1 · Creative Personality Types

Each Personality Type's Way of Living

If you have tried to change your problem with the best intentions and failed, you may think that you are bound to disappointment or to breaking up. Perhaps you feel like a character cast in a play in which you had no say over your role. You wanted to play Cinderella's prince but your wife is responding to you as if you were a ghoulish creature from *The Rocky Horror Picture Show.*

Relationship disappointments can make us feel hopeless, victimized, depressed, and deeply unsettled. Feeling misunderstood or unappreciated is common for many of us, but it no longer need be a routine experience. If you are involved in a relationship conflict that seems unchangeable, familiar as the sunrise, cyclical and predictable as the rotations of a clock, there is a strong chance that you can enter into new and fulfilling territory with your partner.

By taking a creative approach, you can find unexpected surprises and pleasures in your relationship. If you think you are not a creative person, don't worry. Creativity is not confined to the canvas, the stage, or a musical instrument. Building relationship is a work of art in which we all participate.

When you have sincerely attempted to improve your relationship and it is not changing, you may be locked in a particular Creative Personality Type of approach. Each of us falls mainly into one of twelve different Creative Personality Types. By learning the wisdom of the Creative Personality Types, and your own gifts, you can develop your ability to effect a profound change in your relationship. When you begin to understand another's wisdom, it becomes your own.

You are probably wondering which Creative Personality Type am I? These types are quite transparent in the musical theater: Actor, Dancer, Critic, Score Composer, Set Designer, Stage Manager, Playwright, Director, Lighting Designer, Sound Designer, Promoter, and Audience Member. Every member of the theater company provides a valuable contribution without which the play could not be complete. By including the varied intelligences of the different participants in a theater production, all human senses are stimulated. Your relationship-life will be more complete when you communicate with all of your senses. You can learn to do this by drawing upon the knowledge of the Creative Personality Types in daily living.

By understanding more about another's Creative Personality Type, you can improve your relationship with him or her and consequently your relationship with yourself. Each time you make a creative change in your response to another, you add versatility to your responses and to life circumstances. As a result, situations in which you used to feel cast in an unwanted role may become opportunities for a deeper and richer experience of living.

The Actor

The Actor's personality is a great catalyst for change and excitement, contributing emotional zest to every situation. Do you know anyone who has a strong emotional reaction to all kinds of things on a daily basis? Do you have a friend who is at the depths of despair in the morning, and when you call him three hours later to make sure everything is all right, he is in seventh heaven and surprised that you are bringing up an old problem? That's the Actor.

The Actor is both the expresser and the one who makes sure that all feelings are out in the open. This allows us to keep our passion ignited and to approach life with alacrity. The Actor is the personality of climax; every event is an opportunity for peak excitement of one emotion or another. The Actor is elementally a fiery personality.

The Actor in her most evolved state reminds us that all of life's expressions are beautiful and ephemeral tools for connection, while only life itself is eternal. Emotions and thoughts, situations and ranks are forever changing, so the Actor teaches us to make the most of everything through authentic expression. Evolved Actors delight in living the stories of life but are not overly attached to the story lines. The Actor can find deep emotional meaning in any situation.

In his least evolved state, the Actor completely identifies with emotions and thinks there is nothing else. Life becomes a soap opera, and the Actor is the star. When the less evolved Actor is not receiving attention, she is angry. The evolved Actor focuses everyone's attention with an emotional expression and feels alive and content. It is the wisdom of the Actor that we can choose to emulate: freedom of expression. When expression takes place authentically and fully, even the most stubborn conflict will naturally begin to change.

The Dancer

The Dancer's personality is a great asset to the Actor's personality because the Dancer helps life to stay in flux. The Actor ignites passion with outbursts of emotion, and the Dancer embodies that emotion, grounds it, and settles it so that it can flow and change. The Dancer lives life on the level of muscle, bone, and blood but is made of the element water. The human body is composed primarily of water, and the Dancer is the bodily expression of life. The Dancer feels deeply, and in that feeling helps us to feel and find peace with emotions in a human body.

Whereas the Actor is extremely extroverted, the Dancer is more of an introvert. The Dancer experiences life inwardly yet lets us see this process with body movement. Do you know someone who doesn't want to process intellectually about the relationship but offers presence in which change can easily occur if you are patient? That's the Dancer.

In his most evolved state, the Dancer is the essence of motion, unattached to outcomes and highly in tune with the ever-changing feelings of living. Like the seasons, the Dancer is rhythm and flux. Whereas the Actor is spring in bloom, autumn at its colorful peak, summer at its hottest, and winter under ice, the Dancer is transition: seasons moving from one to the other. In her least evolved state, the Dancer is aimless and sorrowful about this. In her most evolved state, she is the nurturer of transition and emanates deep peace.

It is the wisdom of the Dancer that we can choose to emulate: embodied acceptance of who we truly are on the level of our feelings. When we critique, analyze, or over-express our feelings, we lose depth of experience. When we let ourselves feel deeply in every cell of our body and every breath, with or without conflict, there is peace in living.

The Critic

The Critic can be a great help to the Dancer because the Critic's ideals and expectations inspire everyone to do their best. Do you know someone who finds fault with almost everything but never gives up trying to make things better? That's the Critic. No matter how much you practice, how hard you try, and how dedicated you are, the Critic will remind you that perfection has not been reached. The Critic provides keen attentiveness to what is happening and also not happening, here and now. She shows intense drive toward making sure that everyone is involved in realizing these expectations.

In his most evolved state, the Critic calls forth our best and simultaneously is at peace with the fact that we will never reach perfection. The less evolved Critic is frustrated and disappointed with life as it is and, consequently, all other participants. In her evolved state, the Critic is proud and enduring.

We want to utilize the Critic's wisdom of respectfully expecting the best of ourselves and others. This leads to great accomplishments and inspires people to make life the best it can be.

The Score Composer

The Score Composer is a great balance to the Critic. While the Critic focuses on what isn't, the Score Composer dreams and creates with music, focusing upon what can be. The Score Composer is more concerned with lofty visions of world peace and love than what is happening right now at the rehearsal. The Score Composer can feel into states that the heart knows and words cannot describe. The Critic focuses on what everyone could be doing better, while the Score Composer is in a dream world of how life might be. The Score Composer lives in the ether and would prefer to stay there instead of joining in any mundane existence.

The Score Composer creates a world that goes deeper than the human intellect, calling forth feelings of transcendence. Although the Score Composer can express all types of emotion, he is more in tune with the heavenly crib in which these emotions are expressed than the emotions themselves. It is through his medium that we find a deeper level of acceptance with our own experience. The Score Composer dreams of angels and spirits who turn our earthly life into heaven. The Score

Composer takes us into deep fantasy and gives us dreams to wish for, work for, and strive towards.

In her most evolved state, the Score Composer is an inspirer who knows she is here to take humanity to a deeper state of love and connectedness, and she is at peace with her role. She knows she is ahead of her time, and being a servant to humanity, she has no qualms with this. Her music infiltrates people's breath, structure, and existence.

In her least evolved state, the Score Composer expects humanity to rise to the occasion of her delicious tunes, which, of course, we cannot. Thus, he removes himself from society, living in an isolation that vacillates between euphoric fantasy and desperate loneliness.

The Score Composer's wisdom is something we can remember with dreams and meditations. Feeling bliss inwardly and knowing love in fantasy is the source of bringing joy and love into daily life. When we remember what it is that we long for at the core, we stop blaming and look for pathways.

The Set Designer

The Set Designer is a great help to the Score Composer because the designer comes up with plans that bring ideas into life. The Set Designers create the stage so that the world of ideas can come alive in an environment of substance. Do you know someone who likes to build, paint, or construct things? The designer may not do well in a philosophy class because she lives in the world of practicality. The Set Designer is made of earth.

The Set Designer reminds us that life is simple. In his most evolved state, the Set Designer is a hard-working, constructive person who builds whatever is needed. He knows at heart that building is an act of devotion to life, Spirit, and those around him. In his least evolved state, the Set Designer is only concerned with construction, and without a deeper purpose of heart, his work feels empty.

The Set Designer will get depressed when he is not acting in the best interests of a project. When exercising wisdom he is grounded and emanates a sense of security. We can utilize the designer's wisdom when thoughtful solutions yield no constructive changes. Sometimes the answer to a relationship's unsolvable problem is simply to get to work: mow the lawn, paint the house, clean the sink.

The Stage Manager

The Stage Manager is necessary when the Set Designer requires another's help to complete all of her tasks. The Stage Manager shows up when something is needed that no one else plans to do. The Stage Manager reminds us to put purpose before self-centeredness. Do you know someone who calls just when you need a babysitter, runs out from your dinner party to pick up the dessert you forgot, who doesn't specialize in one area but seems to do a million things pretty well? That's the Stage Manager.

The Stage Manager wants to help everyone else and does so. The typos on the program that were discovered when the typesetter was out of town, the flowers for the lobby that were forgotten until the last minute, and the thank-you cards to the donors will always get handled because the Stage Manager will show up to handle them. The Stage Manager has emotional radar that keeps her in close proximity to whatever is needed.

The Stage Manager is like viscoelastic foam, adapting herself quickly to any situation. In her most evolved state, the Stage Manager puts group purpose before individual pursuit and feels grateful for the experience of service. In her least evolved state, she is filled with complaints and low self-esteem, feeling that her little tasks amount to nothing much.

The wisdom we can gather from the Stage Manager is that of gratitude and service. Sometimes a relationship problem can be altered with small acts of kindness and temporarily removing our focus from our own needs.

The Playwright

The Playwright is needed by all of these personalities because he is the one who sees meaning in what is happening and offers a story, which gives sense to our worlds. The Playwright accomplishes this task by using language. The Playwright's medium is words. Do you know someone who provides observations, stories, questions, or meanings? The Playwright is gifted with the ability to interpret. His language defines characters and plots in ways that change our lives.

The Playwright is highly instrumental in helping us redesign areas in which we feel stuck, because she provides us with a new perspective on life's circumstances. The Playwright gives meaning to situations that might otherwise seem confusing.

The Playwright is made of air: ideas. In his most evolved state, the Playwright invites us to look at ourselves positively and with forgiveness. He lets us see who we are with compassion so that we can be at peace about it, or we can accept challenge as an invitation for new learning. In his least evolved state, the Playwright makes numerous comments about what people are doing but derives no conclusion or lesson from his observations. A Playwright in this state feels undernourished and disconnected from humanity. In his evolved state, the Playwright delights in meaningful existence.

The wisdom we can utilize from the Playwright is the willingness to use language constructively. The Playwright teaches us to play with language in order to develop understanding. When two people are in conflict and one has the courage to discuss her own role with new words, there is a strong chance that valuable learning will result.

The Director

The Director is the leader who brings cohesion to all of these personalities. The Director is interested in the overall project. The Director is able to take the talents of the group and celebrate them all. To do this, she must have a bit of earth, water, air, fire, and ether in her style.

Do you know someone who is more talented at pulling together the skills of everyone else than at pursuing his own talent? Actually, this takes the Director's talent. In his most evolved state, the Director is the heart of life, a devoted servant whose soul comes fully alive in the act of enlivening everyone else's personality and soul for a common goal. In his least evolved state, the Director is dedicated to being the boss and is more concerned with maintaining control than demonstrating the gift of empowerment that resides within deep humility. When disempowered, the Director is scornful. When empowered, the Director is made of love.

From the Director we can learn the wisdom of group organization. When the Director is doing a good job, she calls forth everyone's happiness. When power and control issues threaten the well-being of two people in relationship, this ability is important.

The Lighting Designer

The Lighting Designer determines how we see circumstances and people. The Lighting Designer can make a situation appear celebratory or dismal. She can make a person look healthy or ill. The Lighting Designer does not pick the scenery, the people, or the circumstances, but she does affect our perception   by adding or subtracting focus. Do you know someone who can make life seem like a happy event even in the most horrific circumstances? That's the Lighting Designer, who combines the elements air and fire. In her most evolved state, she is the eternal optimist, providing a positive outlook for all those who come in contact with her. In her least evolved state, she is the eternal pessimist, distorting life into a terrible situation.

The Lighting Designer has the ability to take any tragedy and offer a new way of looking at it. A Lighting Designer makes a good catch or consultant because he can pull the value out of the worst of conditions. This is important in relationships because conflict is inevitable. A person who can see the opportunity for growth in a conflict provides the steps for recovery when a relationship is in danger.

In her most evolved state, the Lighting Designer knows human suffering but transcends it. In her least evolved state, the Lighting Designer overlooks suffering, which leads to other difficulties.

From the Lighting Designer we can learn that the stories we live, our life plays, are always opportunities for becoming happier. Ultimately, our love and happiness come from our ability to create them regardless of any circumstances. An evolved Lighting Designer can lead the way.

Although we cannot control every event that happens in our lives, we can choose our perspective. We can make our relationship conflicts hindrances, or we can make them opportunities for positive transformation.

The Sound Designer

The Sound Designer also shapes our perspective. While the Lighting Designer affects what we see in the external world, the Sound Designer affects what we feel inwardly. Do you know someone whose presence commands peace? He walks in the room and people become more settled and happy? That's the Sound Designer, who sets the tone. The Sound Designer uses volume, prerecorded sounds, prerecorded voices, and mood music to establish how we feel about what is happening on stage.

The Sound Designer draws upon feelings that he has previously discovered to affect the mood in a relationship. He can bring deep happiness or deep upset to you without saying a word. You will feel your mood changing without reason when a Sound Designer is present.

Like the Score Composer, the Sound Designer is more tuned into the ethers than the practical world. While the Lighting Designer directs our focus in the practical world, the Sound Designer affects us more subtly. We feel her effect. A Score Composer creates music from feelings within. A Sound Designer recreates moods from feelings she has learned about elsewhere. A Sound Designer in her least evolved state can pull everyone at a family gathering into a state of despair without even opening her mouth. A Sound Designer in her most evolved state can pull everyone at a family gathering up into a state of euphoria.

It is easy to miss the Sound Designer's effects because he operates quietly. He is like a radio transmitter influencing others on how to feel with his moods. In his most evolved state, he provides an aura of joyful serenity. In his least evolved, his strong presence contributes static and chaos to the environment.

In her most evolved state, the Sound Designer will take you to worlds of peace and elation. The Sound Designer is a reminder that there are other worlds besides those of the earth. In her least evolved state the Sound Designer will be spaced out, attracted to worlds outside of the here and now but unable to bring those worlds to others.

From the Sound Designer we learn to focus ourselves inwardly, to turn to our hearts rather than to chaos when a conflict needs a solution.

From the Sound Designer we learn that our private thoughts and feelings have influence on our relationship, as do our outwardly spoken words. The Sound Designer shows us that a relationship conflict can be surprisingly altered by a change in thought.

Try focusing only on the positive aspects of your relationship for a week. Soon your entire being, your aura, your vibration will have a new tone. This tone will affect your partner, and his or her responses are likely to change. This approach is the wisdom of the Sound Designer.

The Promoter

The Promoter is the person who makes sure that the cast's work does not go unnoticed. Gifted with the ability to see what's great about the play, the Promoter's passion comes from enrolling others into seeing the show. Do you know someone who gets hyped up about all kinds of things and has the enthusiasm to get all kinds of other people involved? That's the Promoter. Her medium is enthusiasm.

The Promoter can reach out to anyone from any culture with any type of personality, religious affiliation, or political belief, because the Promoter lives from a universal point of contact: enthusiasm. When things are going badly and someone wants to quit, get a Promoter involved and people will become excited once again.

The Promoter is made of fire. In her most evolved state, the Promoter is pure joy and motivation. In her least evolved state, the Promoter is a salesperson who abandons sight of her role of providing happiness in order to get something from someone. In this least evolved state, she becomes very self-centered and manipulative.

The Promoter teaches us the wisdom of joyful inclusion. When your relationship is full of disappointment, engage each other. Give each other happy attention and watch things change instantaneously.

The Audience Member

The Audience Member is the acknowledger, giving all the personalities the validation that we need. Do you know someone who makes everyone else feel like they belong? The Audience Member is the one who praises, witnesses, and thanks. The Audience Member is the grand receiver, making everyone else's gifts valuable. The Audience Member is made of ether and makes a home for others.

The Audience Member in her most evolved state is very interactive in her observance, valuing all of us for who we are. In her least evolved state, the Audience Member is judgmental and jealous, not fully participating and consequently summing people up and feeling left out. An Audience Member who is on track is a peaceful witness of self and others.

■ ■ ■

By understanding how each of these personality types

approaches a love relationship, we can solve many of our own problems. When both members of a couple dedicate themselves to responding to the other's personality type, the relationship can go through profound and wonderful changes.

When you hold your mate's personality in high regard, your mate becomes happier and has more to give to you. In responding to your mate or any person involved in your life with the wisdom of other personality types, your ability to change a situation expands. You become more in tune with your deepest potential. You experience a new part of yourself, and in doing so find new freedom. You no longer feel like a character cast unwillingly in a role: instead you become a person who is full of endless possibilities.

When you are motivated to make a change but not sure where to start, use the following list to remember your options.

Twelve Types of Wisdom for Improving Communication

- Express your emotions. Be receptive to the other person's emotions. (Actor)
- Be aware of sensations. (Dancer)
- Look for a better method. (Critic)
- Dream of the idyllic. (Score Composer)
- Do something practical. (Set Designer)
- Offer a helping hand to the others involved. (Stage Manager)
- Look for the lesson of life. (Playwright)
- Take both of your needs into account equally. (Director)

- Look for what's already good in the situation.
  (Lighting Designer)
- Create a good feeling within yourself. (Sound Designer)
- Find your enthusiasm. (Promoter)
- Observe in order to build understanding.
  (Audience Member)

■ ■ ■

When you have access to varied responses, circumstances that previously felt trapping begin to feel full of possibilities. When you are able to respond to the same situation with a number of styles, you benefit the most. When you stretch your thinking and behavior, you will find that limits to your love and happiness were imposed by yourself, not by your partner, your parent, your boss, or your next-door neighbor.

When you creatively access new parts of yourself, you find that you are a co-creator in everything you experience, and the other co-creators in your life are here to support you. When the air becomes knotted, and conversation is a snarly mess, free yourself by playfully relaxing into a new approach. Soften the tight trap you have co-created with silky words and sweetly-scented actions. You get to set the stage in your life.

2 · Creative Romance

Improving Sex With Your New Perspectives

Frederick turned to me during the support group meeting and said, "My girlfriend told me that I am not romantic enough. What does romance mean to a woman?"

"Why not ask the women in the group?" I said, so he did.

Juanita answered immediately. "Romance means intimacy and connection, which means paying attention to detail. My husband knows that I like chocolate-covered strawberries and flamenco music. After six years, he still stops at Buckharts to pick up dessert at least once a week. Several times a year, he surprises me with a new CD of the music I love. Last birthday, he said he had a surprise, and we ended up watching a dance concert with my favorite flamenco dancers."

Janet was next. "I also feel that romance stems from intimacy and connection, but for me it's not in gifts. Romance comes in words. I like to hear that I am loved. I like my boyfriend to ask about my day while we make dinner together. I like my boyfriend to tell me what he loves about me while we are making love."

"Romance is communication and connectedness to me also," Shawnice said, "but intimacy goes beyond words. Life is full of intellect. Love life is the one place I can leave my intellect behind and live in the world of feeling. I like to be touched, massaged, and hugged. I can never get enough touch, and touch never ceases to be romantic. It's the most intimate form of connection there is. My girlfriend loves to touch, and this is the most important part of our relationship."

"I like intimacy and excitement," said Angie. "Romance is enhanced by surprise. My boyfriend picked me up at work and had my bike on the rack along with his. He drove me to a hotel in Mendocino, which overlooked the ocean. A candlelight dinner was set up on the balcony. The next morning he took me on a bike ride to a secret place in a private cove where we made love. I was a little nervous that someone would pass by. Nobody did, but the nervousness made our lovemaking ecstatic."

Romance Means Something Different to Each Individual

Each of the Creative Personality Types has unique wisdom to contribute to romance and lovemaking. Lovemaking is communication that occurs all day long, and sex is part of this. When romance and sex are causing you or your partner disappointment, communication is the key. Find out what your partner desires. All of the women in Frederick's relationship group mentioned connection, intimacy, or communication as being paramount in romance. What these words meant to each of these women greatly varied, however, depending upon their Creative Personality Type.

The number one authority on what you desire is you, while the number one authority on what your partner desires is he. However, learning from the wisdom of each personality type can give you new ideas when romance feels stifled or lacking.

One couple turned a very dissatisfying sex life into an electrifying one by inspiring each other with descriptions of their different needs. Understanding how they did this can help you address many types of communication issues that occur in relationships. Alison hungered for the Dancer personality type's version of romance, which emphasizes the pleasure found in flow—the continuous movement from one sensation to another. She also sought pleasure in unexpected surprise, as does the Actor personality type. Her boyfriend, Aaron, experienced sexual pleasure in response to the visual atmosphere, which is what the Lighting Designer personality type does.

Alison was disappointed because her soothing, loving boyfriend didn't enrapture her with a flaming embrace that ignited her dreams when they slept entwined. There was no dramatic flair in her sex life with Aaron. He was too predictable and consistent to satisfy her appetite for variation. She felt he left her with disappointing morning ashes after a little campfire of a sex life. Alison needed to feel lots of motion and change in her love life. "I practically tumble and dance as I make love and need to be matched," she complained. "Aaron is boring when we make love."

Aaron was dissatisfied with his sex life with creative, inspiring Alison. Aaron had made their bedroom into a loving haven. He painted the walls lavender. He adorned the walls with posters of romantic couples. He filled the room with candlelight whenever he wanted to make love. "Alison doesn't care about beauty," he complained. "Alison can make love on the den carpet next to stacks of papers. She doesn't try to make our love life exciting. Alison comes home from the studio in a ragged old T-shirt and tights, and wants to make love. She forgets to shave. I don't find this enticing. I'm wearing silk shirts and tailored trousers when she arrives. I shave my face perfectly and trim my pubic hair. When we first had sex, she had just finished a recital and was wearing a flowing sky blue dress that matched her eyes. After everyone had gone home, we made love on stage with a background of white lace and pink flowers, so I felt the power of my masculinity embraced by her femininity. Our first night was the best."

Alison responded, "When we first made love, I was high from dancing and Aaron tuned into me. We rolled all over the stage. We had gentle moments and animalistic moments, fast motion and slow motion in our lovemaking. We explored every part of each other's bodies. We made love for three hours. I thought he was my perfect sexual match. He was fiery and alive back then, but now he's not at all. We make love sweetly and gently but there's nothing ecstatic about it. He hides his maleness from me now."

Alison and Aaron wanted the same thing but needed to arrive at it differently. Alison was most hungry for flux and movement, which the Dancer personality understands. Aaron was turned on by environment, which a Set Designer personality creates. Alison had a bit of a dramatic flair (the Actor) in her needs. Aaron had a bit of the Critic's perfectionism in his.

Their first night of lovemaking was passionate because Aaron was surrounded with visual beauty and Alison was touched by his choreographic variety. Both were sensually fulfilled. When Alison was alive in her dance and body, she had a lot to give Aaron and felt that he met her. When the visual environment was beautiful to Aaron, he felt excited and nourished.

Alison didn't realize that Aaron's passion relied deeply upon visual environment. Aaron didn't understand that movement was the primary catalyst for Alison's ecstasy. With such different orientations to life, neither truly comprehended the other's needs.

Through ongoing conversations and commitment to their process, Alison and Aaron were able to identify this problem and creatively address it. Aaron did several things to turn his Dancer woman into his dream princess. Before she came home from rehearsals, he lay on his back with favorite music playing and let himself spontaneously flow and move. Tuning into each physical impulse, he found himself moving in ways he never had before and waking up parts of his body that had been asleep. He became more alive in his body. He learned that Alison felt his physical vitality through her skin and deep into her body. Hence, he brought himself to a place of vibrancy before she arrived.

When Aaron heard Alison's car driving up, he practiced the ancient yogic breath of fire. He pushed all of the air out of his belly forcefully using his stomach muscles and then naturally took a quick inhalation. His skin tingled and his body felt alive.

He brought his own masculinity to its peak. Alison, highly sensitive physically, felt and responded delightedly to this.

When Alison arrived, he greeted her at the door and danced with her, moving his limbs all around her, letting his chest touch hers, his stomach slide around her stomach and back, his face move up and down her legs. He brought to their sexual dance the motion she desired. By the time they were kissing he had drawn love designs all over her body with his tongue and touched her from head to toes with his hands. By the time that he was inside of her, his body knew hers as if it were part of his own. His entire body breathed air in and out while he was undulated with the full length of his spine. Alison was ecstatic with her new somatic prince.

Alison fed Aaron's senses, too. He usually left for work and returned before she did. In the morning Alison visually arranged their bedroom haven in a way that Aaron loved. Decorating their bedroom became a creative endeavor. She cut flowers from their garden and put them in vases all over the room, trying different arrangements until the colors fit in a way that felt best. She tidied up. She put candles on windowsills and shelves. Sometimes she bought a new photograph or a painting for their wall. She picked out pretty clothes to bring to work to dress in before coming home. Sometimes she bought him a handsome shirt or piece of jewelry and left it out for him, then arrived home in a matching outfit. Her partner's attentiveness to visual detail inspired her. The Dancer began to find joy in helping make the set. Alison showed Aaron that she loved his body by trimming his hair, moving her eyes over his delicious body during sex, and complimenting his carefully chosen clothes. Aaron was elated with his sexy beauty.

Alison and Aaron turned around their sex life by using visual art and dance in living. Often we get trapped in cycles of disappointment and complaining instead of simply asking for what we want in direct, concise terms. We think our partner should know what we want if we say, "I want to be loved passionately and intimately." If they really love us, we tell ourselves, they should know what we think, but this isn't so.

As exemplified by Alison and Aaron, we are all very different in our needs. Communication is the core of a good relationship, and sex and communication take place in many forms. By understanding each of the personality types in relationship, romance, and sexuality, we can enrich our lives. Find out from your partner what makes him or her happy.

The Actor in Romance

At the beginning of this chapter, the Actor's contribution to romance is eloquently expressed by Angie's description of her surprise trip to Mendocino. Her boyfriend, the Actor, was skilled at creating high drama with a memorable surprise. The Actor likes to stir the emotions, and an evolved Actor will build situations that lead to ecstasy. An unconscious Actor might stir things up with a fight or a self-pity fit. If someone is behaving as an unevolved Actor, assume that she desires drama but needs your assistance in creating it in a positive way.

The Actor likes to stimulate intense emotion with variation. She might take you to a fancy restaurant on the town one night and a campsite in the wilderness the next. The Actor can be found entertaining her lover with different accents, dramatic greetings, and shocking conversations, because everything the Actor does is pointed towards producing emotional expression.

The Actor offers spontaneity. I will never forget my ex-boyfriend, an Actor and Dancer Creative Personality Type, who gave me exquisite joy when he ran down the airport hall to pick me up and twirled me around and around. When an Actor friend went to Venezuela with his Actor girlfriend, deep-sea diving fifty feet under water they spontaneously decided to take a breath, remove their regulators, and give each other a kiss.

The Actor will find all kinds of places to make love to you: the kitchen, on top of the washing machine, in the closet while you are on a ladder fixing a light bulb. The Actor likes risk and may invite you to make love on the beach under a towel or in the airplane bathroom, or in the hot tub while it just looks like you are standing behind her and no one can really tell.

The Actor will throw a kiss to you in the middle of a serious dinner discussion at the relatives' and do it in such a way that everyone notices. He will call you during the workday and ask your secretary to say it's an emergency. Then he will sing "You Are the Sunshine of My Life" on the phone. She may show up at your office in a silk gown with a huge bouquet of flowers and whisper a love poem in your ear. When you are in love with an Actor, expect emotional adventure and surprise.

The Dancer in Romance

The Dancer loves touch. The Dancer likes to kiss with toes, hug with all limbs, dance with tongues. The Dancer will turn you on in every nook and cranny of her body. She will find you to be like thirty-one flavors of ice cream. Every part of you is a special flavor. She can orgasm in her heart, she can feel ecstasy in her tummy, she can well up with excitement in her throat. He will do everything he can to give such experiences to you. He will find ways to touch, massage, kiss, cuddle, and stroke every part of your body, and he wants to share with you every part of his body as well. She will wrap her limbs around you, lie on top of you, put her cheek next to yours, and swirl around you like a snake while she runs her fingers through your hair, finding endless ways to physically connect.

The Dancer likes to move in all types of ways. One moment she is a graceful ballerina, and the next she is a strong African Dancer. She will roll and tumble with you. The Dancer likes to tumble and play and literally dance while making love. This keeps her alive and turns her on.

The Dancer can survive on a menu of different sensations quite blissfully. He will bring all different types of touch to you: light butterfly, soft stroking, medium muscle massaging, firm hugging, strong holding. He may be very sensitive or very earthy or something in between.

The Dancer loves to feel the sensations of the environment, as well as your body. She may take you for a barefoot walk in the sand, visit the hot springs, swim with you while hugging you in the bay or ocean or pool, slide down a water slide, take a mud bath, get flannel sheets and satin covering for your bed, dress in soft silk pajamas, and warm the massage oil in the sun or on the stove to caress your body.

She may invite you to take a warm bath and dry you off with the softest towels she can find, roll with you on a sheepskin carpet, make love in the tall grass, and try out a hundred different positions. When you date a Dancer get ready to swim in a sea of sensory experiences.

The Critic in Romance

The Critic wants everything to be at its best, so he will constantly bring up improvements that are needed in your love life. He will bring home books and videos, comment on what friends said about their love life, and initiate improvement discussions. She will address all areas of your lovemaking in terms of what she liked and what can be better. She will discuss every aspect of romance and sex in terms of creating the perfect love life, expecting both of you to work at these improvements with devotion.

If you can get past feeling berated by the Critic's constant feedback, you will discover that her ideas can enhance your love life greatly. If you work with the Critic, she will be happy and forgiving and deeply accept all imperfections. If you resist her, she will multiply the complaints until you can't stand it anymore.

From the Critic we can learn to step outside of ourselves and view our situation from a distance, noting what we do well and what can be improved. When we are humble enough to do this, we will experience worlds we would never otherwise have had access to. When you are involved with a Critic get ready to hear an ongoing critique about what works and what doesn't.

The Score Composer in Romance

The Score Composer is turned on by sound. She will take you to concerts, fill your home with music, and turn on a CD when you are having sex. She will point out the passion inspired by natural sound when she takes you to hear the ocean waves or the crickets by a lake. The Score Composer will lead you to reach for the stars because she is focused on experience that sublimates words.

The Score Composer can become highly attentive to what kind of sounds fill life, for sounds pull us out of the mundane and into the world of inspiration and fantasy. He desires a blissful experience that can only be found in feeling, and his gateway to feeling is through his heart and ears. He is likely to live somewhere that is surrounded by beautiful sounds and if he must be near ugly sounds (traffic, lawn mowers, other noisy machines) he will become cranky and grumpy.

The Score Composer responds to your voice. How loved she feels is related to the tone of your voice. "I love you" means nothing if it isn't said with warmth. Anger and shrillness in your voice can deeply trouble the Score Composer. I dated a Score Composer who could comfort me if I showed an angry face but would choose to get off the phone if I sounded irritated.

The Score Composer feels sound throughout his entire body. Feel free to express moans and sighs from the core of your soul to your Score Composer. He loves to hear you. You never need to be embarrassed with your most spontaneous animalistic voices when making love with the Score Composer. His passion for you grows deeper with each of your sighs. Let him know you want to hear his moans and sighs, too. Tell him frequently, "Oh baby, I love hearing your voice."

The Score Composer will find any occasion to add a sound that is soothing or exciting to your home and get rid of sounds that aren't. Choose the alarm clock with the beautiful bell, the car with the purr, the stereo with the best sound that you can afford. To her it's worth the splurge. If your love is a Score Composer, you will be invited into the world of idealism and sound.

The Set Designer in Romance

The Set Designer is interested in making sure that everyone and everything is well taken care of. When everyone has eaten, the house is clean, the bills are paid, and the garden is watered, the Set Designer feels good and whole, and romance and love with her is secure and nurturing.

The Set Designer is especially attentive to how the environment affects each of the senses. For example, life needs to smell good. The Set Designer will buy an air machine to make sure that the air is fresh, or he will take you to Hawaii to get the best air you can find. He will burn delicious incense, spray you with herbal mist, wear unusual perfumes and lotions, serve teas with sweet, memorable fragrances, and only pick a lover who naturally smells appealing to him.

Sex feels good when the atmospheric surroundings feel good. The Set Designer will make sure that you have a comfortable bed and appealing interior decorations. The house temperature will be important to her, as will be eating good food. This is the source of a sexy life with the Set Designer.

The Set Designer provides a nourishing environment, which is something that we all need. When romance feels lacking in passion, use the Set Designer's wisdom to make the environment appealing. When affection does not suffice as nourishment, draw upon the Set Designer's awareness to make sure that the interior decorations are contributing to rather than inhibiting your sense of well-being. When you marry a Set Designer, you will be provided with many external comforts.

The Stage Manager in Romance

The Stage Manager is turned on when he knows that he is contributing. Mistakenly criticized for being "co-dependent", the Stage Manager is actually a person who cares about others' well-being. He will remember to blow the candles out before you go to sleep. He will get up to get water for both of you after you make love. He will cover your feet with a blanket if your toes are cold. The Stage Manager loves to make you happy.

Paying attention to details is important to the Stage Manager. She notices whatever it is that needs to be done and does it. Each Stage Manager will draw significantly upon the other personality types in terms of her romantic desires. What is most important to her, however, is that she serves you. Whether one's service is in a somatic, auditory, or visual style is secondary to the fact that he or she serves. When he has ways to give, the Stage Manager is carefree and satisfied.

If he is not received with gratitude, the Stage Manager will often withdraw.

We can all learn from Stage Managers because they do not put themselves first. In a self-centered culture, people like this are often pathologized. If everyone in our culture were a Stage Manager, however, we would come to see that their behavior is developmentally that of an adult, while we are still valuing adolescent behavior as a cultural norm. When you fall in love with a Stage Manager, you can expect to be generously served.

The Playwright in Romance

Conversations are important to Playwrights. They ask questions, offer insights, and derive meanings that keep conversations interactive. Playwrights can talk descriptively about situations and feelings. They know life to be a series of interesting stories. The Playwright thrives on words. She will compliment you frequently with poetic language or detailed observations that you will remember. Playwrights can fill your heart with love made out of words.

The Playwright will whisper romantic thoughts to you when making love. He will say something precious when you orgasm. He will make sweet comments when you hold each other after sex.

She will leave poems on the door, in your briefcase, on your car seat. You may find a quote from one of her favorite poets hidden in your dinner napkin or rolled into a scroll and tied to your toothbrush. She will take you to lectures, book readings, and poetry readings. She will point to lyrics in the program while you're listening to a concert.

He will be creative in answering questions. The Playwright enjoys the discovery and passing back and forth of words. A new word is like a surprise package. Your Playwright may put a book under your pillow. He may build up to a passionate evening by calling you at work and verbally presenting alluring sexual fantasies. Your Playwright lover will offer you seductive stories and pleasing tales.

The Director in Romance

The Director is more concerned with the way in which the two of you are relating than her needs alone. How you felt about the way you touched her and how she touched you in response is more important to the Director than her solo needs. How you felt when he said what he thought about what you wore is something the Director will think about. To the Director, every situation is an intricate result of the causes and effects of all personalities and the environment involved.

The Director looks at everyone and the many different ways that they are involved. If either of you is upset, the Director will work overtime to brings things to cohesion. When both of you are happy, the Director is happy. So if your sex life is affected by some incompletion with your last love, the Director is bound to pull this information out of you and feel troubled until you have cleared it up. "We all win or we all lose" is the Director's stance.

We want to emulate Directors because they consider everyone's needs. Their pitfall can be going overboard instead of just letting life be. Like the Critic, the Director is an idealist. The Director will work to make sense out of a situation. If you choose a Director for a mate, your needs will always be considered equally important to hers.

The Lighting Designer in Romance

The Lighting Designer's passion is affected by what she sees. Visually based, the Lighting Designer makes choices about what to feast her eyes upon. She will call attention to things and can make you feel beautiful and delicious when she does. She will notice your body as though it is an art piece, delighting in a haircut and inspiring you with compliments about clothes. She will point out that the shade with which she has polished her toenails is joyous, praise you for keeping yourself in shape, and delight in artistic grooming and shaving.

He will pay attention when you are dressed in exquisite clothes with calming colors to appeal to his peaceful desires and in richer colors to call forth his passion. Your Lighting Designer always notices details like buttons, hairpieces, jewelry, shoes, night wear, clothes for all seasons. What you wear in the morning, in the swimming pool, at the dinner table, or at the gym, is all part of a creative offering in the Lighting Designer's eyes, and he will utilize what he sees to either build sensual well-being or take away from it.

The type of lighting in a room, the color of the walls, the style of furniture, the rugs, and the windows will never go unnoticed by the Lighting Designer. She is quick to observe and be thankful for a new bouquet, painting, beautiful pieces to add to the decor, a mirror on the ceiling.

He will comment on how the dinner is arranged. If he prepares dinner, he will enjoy making the food attractive. Perhaps he will design the salad like a collage, making sure to include every color of the rainbow on the menu.

If she leaves a love note, she will put it on stationery that is art in itself, making her handwriting exquisite or choosing an alluring font.

The Lighting Designer is nourished by beauty. Stray clutter, paper on the rug, hair in the sink makes him feel awful. What he sees resonates deep inside him. He feels he is what he sees. He will redesign what he doesn't like.

The Lighting Designer sees the artwork in the human body. The curves in your body from a distance and the beauty of your body up close in many different positions bring pleasure to the Lighting Designer, so she may ask you to pose. She will look right into your eyes, taking note of the color.

The Lighting Designer teaches us to be attentive to the visuals in our environment. In doing this we can create a world of beauty. If you go out with a Lighting Designer you will be offered many opportunities to feast your eyes.

The Sound Designer in Romance

The Sound Designer can pull you into worlds you never knew existed. When you make love with a Sound Designer, you will find the magic of dreamtime, discover meditation worlds in real life, and realize that fairy tales are as real as daily living.

Once you enter the psychic realms of the Sound Designer, you will know that the wall between inner and outer life is transparent. You may wonder if the wall between heaven and earth is as well. The Sound Designer relies on psychic channels as much as most of us rely on more tangible ones. Don't be surprised if a Sound Designer calls you on the phone immediately after you fantasize about making love to her. If she answers a question of yours that you never said out loud, you know she is a true Sound Designer.

She can guide you into a world of feelings that are different than emotional ones. After you make love with a Sound Designer you will feel like you have gone deep under the sea and learned to swim among mermaids or traveled high in the sky among eagles. Earth life will never again completely quench your thirst. When your honey is a Sound Designer, sexuality and spirituality will be one and the same.

The Promoter in Romance

In the Promoter's eyes, life is an opportunity to get pumped up and enthusiastic, and sex is another thing to get excited about.

"You're a great kisser."

"Wow, I really know how to meet your needs."

"We were meant for each other. We are soul mates for sure!"

"Maybe we should teach tantra workshops. We're so good at sex together!"

The Promoter finds everything to be an occasion to praise and promote.

When praising and promoting, the Promoter is full of joy. If you don't go along with her joy, she will become very unsettled and lost. The wisdom we can take from the Promoter is that of looking for what is good, great, and wonderful in our romantic life and expressing this out loud to our partners and to others, creating security and self-love for everyone. When done in a way that celebrates everyone's goodness as opposed to one-upmanship, this trait makes life happy. If your Promoter partner accepts your marriage proposal, the incredible stories you hear about your own love life will be uplifting.

The Audience Member in Romance

The Audience Member is the witness graciously accepting an experience for what it is. The Audience Member does not evaluate but makes peace with all feelings, thoughts, and experiences, embracing everything as worthy of attention. The Audience Member will experience the physical sensations, the emotional flow, the words exchanged in your conversations in a very present way, deeply involved, uninterested in what might be better or worse about it, and greatly appreciative. The Audience Member is like a Buddha reminding us of life beyond ego, embracing whatever comes with a thankful heart. From the Audience Member's wisdom, we learn to deeply experience life without judging or changing. In this way we remember the fulfillment that babies and animals know in simple existence. When an Audience Member loves you, you can relax in a feeling of deep acceptance.

Three Ways to Deliciously Electrify Your Romance

- Share your feelings and thoughts openly.
- Find out what turns your partner on specifically and try it out.
- Draw upon each of the Creative Personality Types' unique form of wisdom.

■ ■ ■

When you treat each day as an opportunity for discovery, romance and sex become fun and vivacious. Think of every encounter with your beloved as a romantic excursion. Sexual conversation is not limited to the bedroom. All day long you are in a dance of the heart and of sexuality.

Allow life to moisten your lips. Let your lips tell stories. Your stories will fill your lover's chest; soften as they drop into his abdomen, leave words in his groin. His orgasm will be your shared history of adventures breathed in, liquefied, and spilled out in celebration.

3 · Creative Communication

Growing Closer and Happier When Conflict Arises

Now that you are informed about Creative Personality Types, you can use this knowledge to address communication difficulties. This chapter will guide you to approach stale problems with a fresh attitude. A formula designed to make communication constructive and easy is outlined in the following pages. This powerful formula can lead you to success when used to resolve any type of communication problem.

When you are locked in a seemingly insoluble struggle with a partner, you will need to become aware of your partner's positive motive. When your focus is limited to your own desire, you will continue to butt heads. If you refer to the Director's knowledge, assuming that your partner's goal and your goal are equally important, you will be better situated to create a working compromise.

When an argument seems imminent, take some time to explore your own feelings. If you have not found an appropriate outlet for your emotions, anger, blame, and tension are likely to build between you and your partner. Use the Dancer's advice.

Do something physical by yourself before discussing the problem with your partner.

Bring your best of moods to the situation. Emulating the Sound Designer, find a good feeling to bring to your partner. This will make you feel lighthearted about your situation so that you can play with it rather than sink in it.

Remember that disappointment is an invitation to improve the situation. Learn from the Critic. Take all information you have about what isn't working as impetus to make it better.

Rewrite the story you have invented about the situation. Rewrite your role as well. By following in the footsteps of the Playwright, you can describe your situation in a manner that moves you toward new learning and insight. By changing your own role you change your life play.

Taking your focus off what's wrong and centering it on what's needed is your next step. By accessing the Lighting Designer's abilities you can choose where you place your focus. Decide to focus on your needs rather than your dissatisfactions. Look at all the ways in which your partner has been good to you. In addition, activate the Lighting Designer within yourself, by turning your perspective toward gratitude. This will automatically orient you toward solutions and good feelings.

Simplify your understanding of what it is you want and what your partner wants by bringing in the Score Composer's perspective. The Score Composer reduces a dream to its simplest form. Reduce each of your needs to their simplest forms. You may refer to the chart in this chapter to help you do this.

Rather than entangling yourself in an argument, provide ample time for focusing on each of you separately. Remember the Actor's emphasis on expression. Each of you needs to express your basic desire.

Listen to each other without defending or reacting. Turn to the Audience Member for adequate role modeling. Listen to your partner with the intention of receptively hearing his or her request.

Call upon the Set Designer's willingness to build a new environment. Figure out what you can do that will satisfy your partner's hunger as well as your own.

Approach the circumstances with alacrity. Adopt the Promoter's attitude when you discuss your conflicts so that you can generate a sense of joy. Working out problems is fun when you can trust that pleasurable solutions will follow.

Remember that helping each other will lead to deeper love. Find the Stage Manager aspect of yourself so that you become helpful rather than antagonistic.

The above can be combined into eight basic steps.

Eight Practices that Successful People Use to Solve Communication Conflicts

1 Remain solution-oriented at all times.
2 Aim to satisfy your partner's needs as well as your needs.
3 Before addressing the problem with your partner, express your emotions through a physical activity on your own.
4 Clarify both of your needs in simplest terms (one or two words).

5 Practice listening to and receiving your partner's communication with respect.

6 Be playful, fun, and positive. Humor is a good thing!

7 Change your role in the scene you have co-written.

8 Maintain a perspective of gratitude.

Solution-Oriented Formula Used to Turn Chronic Dissatisfaction into Pleasure

When communicating about a problem there is a particular method that will help you to bypass defensiveness, arguing, and withdrawal, thus arriving at a solution rather than a chronic disagreement. The Set Designer, Audience Member, Playwright, Director, and Promoter are experts at solution-oriented communication. The following formula is based on their wisdom and is highly effective.

Give up the complaint. Trade it in for a solution-directed statement. Instead of continuing to say, "I don't want _____" or "I don't like _____," say, "I like _____" or "I love _____." This way you invite your partner to do what you like rather than invite him to defend himself for having done what you disliked.

Point out what you appreciate about your partner in the same conversation. Say "thank you for _____."

Someone who feels appreciated is more willing to participate in a constructive way.

Communicate your willingness to take responsibility in the situation rather than focusing only on your partner. Say, "I am going to address my role in this matter by changing my behavior in the following ways: _____."

Leave out words that put you or your partner down. There is no need to call either of you names or insinuate that you are bad people. Successful people make many mistakes along the way. The fact that you are choosing to make a change shows that you have strong character and good motives. Use words that celebrate your goodness. Say, "We're doing a good job!"

It is quite common to get lost in the frustration of an argument and forget about your original motive as well as to misinterpret your partner's original motive. What is important, however, is that you design a solution. Any problem that you are experiencing in your relationship with a significant other contains an important desire and type of fear. For example, the desire for improvements plus fear will lead to perfectionism while the desire for improvements plus love will lead to contribution. By identifying the basic desire that is being tampered with by your fear and adding love instead, you will be able to change the situation.

In relationships, it is easy to forget that both people involved want something good. When your partner's actions, feelings, or words do not address your immediate desire, you might misinterpret your partner's motives. On the other hand, finding out what your partner desires can lead to a quick solution. When love is consistently added to motives, an experience of transcendence or spirituality is likely to follow.

■ ■ ■

The following charts show you what you will create when you mix a specific motive with fear, love, or ongoing love. When you are lost in a problem, refer to the chart to remember what it is that you truly seek.

The Actor

Desire for:	+ Fear =	+ Love =	+ Interaction =
Recognition	Withdrawal	Spontaneity	Trust in life
Under-standing	Jealousy	Communi-cation	Trust in people
Acknow-ledgment	Narcissism	Self-Expression	Trust in self
Received Expression	Anger	Happiness	Humility

The Dancer

Desire for:	+ Fear =	+ Love =	+ Interaction =
Good Feelings	Numbness	Alertness	Vitality
Pleasure	Addiction	Health	Ecstasy

The Critic

Desire for:	+ Fear =	+ Love =	+ Interaction =
Excellent Circumstances	Arrogance	Encouragement	Inspiration
Improvements	Perfectionism	Contribution	Evolution
Modifications	Frustration	Inclusion of Others	Optimism
Perfection	Hostility	Forgiveness	Satisfaction

The Score Composer

Desire for:	+ Fear =	+ Love =	+ Interaction =
Heaven on Earth	Isolation	Creation	Spirituality
Transcendence	Rejection	Meditation in living	Grace
Euphoria	Escape	Joy	Celebration
Enlightenment	Deprivation	Devotion	Inner/Outer Bridge
Union	Deceit	Communication	Connection

The Set Designer

Desire for:	+ Fear =	+ Love =	+ Interaction =
Comfort	Complaining	Nourishment	Well-being
Security	Greed	Attentiveness	Satisfaction

The Stage Manager

Desire for:	+ Fear =	+ Love =	+ Interaction =
Belonging	Ostentatious Help	Service	Generosity

The Playwright

Desire for:	+ Fear =	+ Love =	+ Interaction =
Resolution	Conflict	Positivity	Peace
Insight	Condemnation	Understanding	Compassion
Purpose	Confusion	Direction	Success
Meaning	Disappointment	Gratitude	Fulfillment

The Director

Desire for:	+ Fear =	+ Love =	+ Interaction =
Community	Control	Leadership	Surrender
Productivity	Bossiness	Accomplishment	Will

The Lighting Designer

Desire for:	+ Fear =	+ Love =	+ Interaction =
Beauty	Pessimism	Exaltation	Awe

The Sound Designer

Desire for:	+ Fear =	+ Love =	+ Interaction =
Inner Harmony	Eeriness	Warmth	Sweetness
Enjoyed Moods	Clash	Inner Pleasure	Serenity

The Promoter

Desire for:	+ Fear =	+ Love =	+ Interaction =
Enthusiasm	Imposition	Delight	Exuberance
Excitement	Artificiality	Fun	Play
Participation	Force	Invitation	Enrollment

The Audience Member

Desire for:	+ Fear =	+ Love =	+ Interaction =
Peace	Superiority	Observation	Awareness
Acceptance	Awkwardness	Support	Appreciation

Dissatisfaction has a big stomach, a slow metabolism, and the capacity to become extremely overweight very fast. The more complaints you feed it, the more power it assumes over your life. Anyone who is overweight and undernourished begins with a healthy desire and a natural hunger to be fed. So it is with your relationship desires and complaints. Dissatisfaction just needs proper nutrition. Finding the positive motives at the core of a communication struggle and addressing these new ways will leave you feeling satiated and pleased.

Remember gratitude in your heart at all times. Each night before you go to sleep, remember something about your partner that nourishes you, something that gives you the opportunity to grow, and something you admire. Tell your partner and enjoy the blossoming love. Initial love comes in a second and is born of grace. Lasting love takes practice and is born of heart-felt wisdom. Eat the moist fruits of love. Drink the sweet nectar of positivity. Wipe your mouth with the clean napkin of attentiveness, and you will dine at the elegant table of ultimate satisfaction.

4 · Creative Self-Care

Becoming the Source of Your Own Happiness

Sometimes learning about your partner's Creative Personality Type isn't enough to solve a conflict. Making sure that he knows about yours is not always enough, either. When your disappointment is not solved by a solution created between you and your partner, it is important to learn how to be responsible for your own happiness. Brenda was irate at her boyfriend because he spent so much of their time together at the gym talking to other women in the sauna room. Brenda realized that her boyfriend wasn't going to change and that he wasn't violating their relationship in any way. He simply liked to talk to lots of people. As an Actor personality type, it was important to him to express himself to others. Nevertheless, her anger felt out of control. She was suffering from it.

Knowing herself to be a Dancer personality type, Brenda believed that physical contact with her boyfriend would eliminate the sorrow she felt when he was talking away in the sauna room. She asked him to make a point to hold her hand or put his arm around her when they were in the sauna so that she wouldn't feel left out. He was happy to oblige, desiring that Brenda be happier during their visits to the gym. Brenda came to me confused about herself because this solution didn't change her feelings. She continued to feel distraught.

I asked Brenda, "What are you missing?"

She burst into tears. "I need something but I don't know what it is."

When you long for something intangible, something that no one else is fulfilling for you, it is time to learn to care for yourself more deeply. Sometimes in life, you feel that something is missing but you cannot identify what it is. In this situation, find a place where you can sit quietly by yourself, talk to a trusted friend, or engage in a creative endeavor. Explore the unmet need. Ask the need, "How old are you? What do you want?" Let the answers come in whatever way they can—thoughts, images, words, or feelings. Spend some time each day exploring this need for two weeks or longer.

After you have discovered more about your need, you can learn to respond to your own need. Take some time to imagine an ideal parent who knows exactly how to respond to this need. You can do this by sitting quietly, and perhaps using music, candles, inspirational tapes, or a natural setting to enter an intimate place with yourself. When your body relaxes and your thoughts slow down, ask your unconscious mind to bring you an unconditionally loving parent within yourself. This parent will know exactly what you need at all times. Allow your imagination to bring forth this parent. You can further develop this parent by painting or drawing him/her, dancing as him/her, speaking his/her words in front of a mirror, introducing him/her to a friend, writing about or as him/her, singing as him/her, observing him/her in your visualization, and asking him/her for support. Remember that s/he is the perfect parent and will give to you in any way you ask.

When Brenda did so, she realized that she lacked confidence in reaching out to others. During her loving-parent meditation she saw herself crying to her perfect mother, telling her, "I want to feel included in the sauna." By allowing herself to fantasize in a relaxed state she found out that her suffering was coming from something different than she originally assumed. Brenda imagined a perfect mother who helped her to feel safe about socializing in public situations.

When Brenda paid attention to her own needs rather than her boyfriend's behavior, she discovered that her insecurity was being escalated by her focus. Using the wisdom of the Lighting Designer, she realized that she was staring at women's breasts and hips in the sauna instead of looking at their faces or her boyfriend. When she readjusted her focus she realized that her boyfriend was very engaged in interesting conversations. His attention was much more on what he was saying than on the women's bodies. In fact, he was looking at the sauna stove much of the time that he spoke. He was involved with expressing himself.

Using the Playwright's wisdom, Brenda realized that she was making up stories about her boyfriend's involvement with other women. After she changed her visual focus, she went on to change the stories. She told herself that her boyfriend was enjoying conversation with others. Soon she realized that she felt isolated and wanted more contact with others. Instead of suffering because of her boyfriend's response to his own needs for expression, she began to engage with the other people in the sauna room and to feel good inside. She began to feel peaceful with her boyfriend's actions because she became focused on meeting her own needs.

Interestingly, when she felt fine about his actions and let go of her psychic grip on him, he spoke a lot less to other women in the sauna and focused on her. When you choose to take care of yourself more deeply, others often respond in surprising ways. Unexpected gifts will arrive but don't stop taking care of yourself. When you begin to depend on gifts for your well-being, you will return to the strain of feeling unmet needs.

The process of re-parenting yourself will allow you to heal old hurts, fill empty holes, and become more secure within yourself. When you feel more secure within yourself, it is easier to ask others for what you need without being dependent upon the answer.

If you find it challenging to clarify your need or to respond to the need, you can gather information from one of the other Creative Personality Types. Each is an expert on how to fulfill one of humanity's needs.

Personality Types' Knowledge About Human Needs

Because most people are predominantly one or two personality types, it is helpful to consider all of them to identify what is missing in you. Then you can give yourself the gift of what you need.

The Actor's Knowledge About Your Needs

The Actor is wise about expression. She says that authentic expression is the key to feeling alive and whole. Speak your truth, share yourself, and do not attempt to be anyone but who you truly are. Do not try to fit yourself into any "should". Just express your feelings and thoughts in whatever form makes you happy, and do it in front of others who have the capacity to enjoy you.

The Dancer's Knowledge About Your Needs

The Dancer is wise about feelings and sensation, believing them all to be fine. Do not criticize, fight, flee, or ignore your feelings. Just feel them like the seasons traveling through. Focus your full heart, body, and mind on any feeling you have. Accept your feeling as though you were arms cradling a child. The more you allow yourself to feel, the more at peace you will be.

The Critic's Knowledge About Your Needs

The Critic is wise about doing one's best. He says that you won't have clarity unless you do whatever task is at hand as best you can. Do a good job for the sake of making life good. Don't attach your worth to how good a job you do. Think of doing a good job as a way of serving a greater purpose. Do your best for Spirit and those around you as an act of devotion to living. Do not do your best merely for recognition. Do your best because in doing so you will find great clarity and abundance.

The Score Composer's Knowledge About Your Needs

The Score Composer is wise about dreaming. She says that dreaming keeps you youthful. When you dream you are reborn. You have the opportunity to dream with each breath. Dream to stay in touch with Spirit. Dream to carry life forward. Dream to remember what and who you truly are. Dream to stay connected with your goodness.

The Set Designer's Knowledge About Your Needs

The Set Designer is wise about being practical. He says that being practical is the source of our well-being and nurture. He says that in order to be happy you must attend to the environment. Make physical improvements wherever you are, and you will feel content.

The Stage Manager's Knowledge About Your Needs

The Stage Manager is wise about supporting others. She says that generosity is the key. Nobody can master a divine quality such as love, gratitude, or compassion without including others. We learn to be whatever it is that we give. Give that which you seek, and your soul will be full of it.

The Playwright's Knowledge About Your Needs

The Playwright is clever with writing her own stories. Write a story about your life that delights you. Your life story is in your own hands.

The Lighting Designer's Knowledge About Your Needs

The Lighting Designer is optimistic. She says whatever you cast your light upon, you will identify as reality. The world is full of many things, yet it is what you choose to shed your light on that prospers. Choose good things upon which to shed your light and you shall prosper.

The Sound Designer's Knowledge About Your Needs

The Sound Designer is wise about creating mood. We can alter the same scenario with love or with fear, depending upon what we bring to it. The Sound Designer says bring your best to each situation. Hear through the ears of love, and love will fill your belly and soul. Listen to yourself with love to start.

The Promoter's Knowledge About Your Needs

The Promoter is wise about informing others of how good people are. When we gossip, we spread bad feelings among community. When we spread the best about others, everyone thrives. The Promoter says, "Tell stories of each other's good qualities, and like garden flowers, these qualities shall grow. Tell yourself good stories about yourself to start."

The Audience Member's Knowledge About Your Needs

The Audience Member is wise about witnessing. Watch yourself and others with no critique. Just watch like a baby watches. Watch to know. Watch yourself to know yourself, and you will feel accepted.

Mending Hurts from Previous Developmental Stages

You have parts of yourself that come from different developmental periods in your life. By getting to know these parts of you, previously uncontrollable disappointments can be transformed. Brenda decided to focus on the needs of the little baby, the little girl, and the teenage self within her. Every time she felt upset with her boyfriend, she asked each of her selves about their needs. Adult Brenda gave baby Brenda, child Brenda, and teenage Brenda whatever they asked for. When she took better care of herself, her boyfriend's care for her became more apparent. When he didn't respond to her in ways she desired, it was not so upsetting because she could respond to herself.

When you go through the re-parenting process, you can switch between responding to your inner baby, your inner child, and your inner teenager. When you identify which part of you is dissatisfied, you can attend to emotions that cannot always be addressed by adult rationality or expectations.
Continuously ask the cast of characters (your inner selves) to help decide who most needs attention. Create two inner parents for them: a mom and a dad. Each day you can get to know one of the characters better by choosing one of the Creative Personality Type's instructions. Ask your inner cast questions that will help you understand and respond to them through the different personality types' eyes. For example, when utilizing the Dancer's wisdom with your inner baby, ask how she feels. The baby won't yet have words, so she will show you. When accessing the knowledge of the Sound Designer ask your inner selves if they are replicating unwanted moods that they learned from others. Ask them if they would like to copy other more pleasing moods. If this process doesn't come naturally, try journal writing or one of the arts to help or switch to your inner child or teenager.

Map to Inner Happiness

- Know what it is that you desire in very clear terms.
- Get to know your inner baby, inner child, and inner teenager.
- Know what your inner baby, child, and teenager need.
- Respond to your inner baby, child, and teenager as a loving parent.
- Use wisdom of the Creative Personality Types to help you clarify your own desires.
- Forgive anyone who didn't know what you needed when you wished they did.
- Offer gratitude to all who have tried to give to you.
- Offer gratitude to your inner baby, child, teenager, and parent.
- Offer gratitude to yourself.
- Offer gratitude to life.
- Offer gratitude to anyone else within your own heart.

The world is a stage on which we create a life play, and this play begins in our psyche. Create a loving relationship with yourself, and you will only care to create the same with others. When you give strength to trouble rather than love, trouble takes over. You get lost in a jungle of words that can strangle you. Vines of dissatisfaction can become so tightly matted to one another that you lose sight of your desired destination. You become entangled with yourself. Your actions clash with your own hopes. When you don't know what you need, your requests screech like lost birds caught in a net.

Wouldn't it make more sense to plant bougainvillaea? Life needs water. Water yourself with care. Words need air between them. Breathe into yourself and discover your own requests. Give vitamins to your desires so that they grow in health. Speak your desires lovingly, and you will fill others' ears with sweetly-scented opportunities to deliciously give.

5 · Creative Empowerment

Knowing Your Life Purpose

It is important to learn how to feed ourselves and be the source of our own joy. In many peoples' lives, however, there comes a time at which pleasing ourselves is not enough. As part of a family as well as a larger world community, each person has an inherent desire to serve others. When you accept a role that allows you to utilize Spirit's gifts to you as your gifts to others, you will feel confident and more complete. In order to do this you need to clarify what your life's purpose is. When you know your life's purpose, and allow it to guide you, you become an empowered person.

If you are unsure about what your life's purpose is, there are ways to find out. First, think about times in life when you have been the happiest. Ask yourself each personality's questions about when you were the happiest.

The Creative Personality Types' Questions for Clarifying Your Life Purpose

The Actor's Life Purpose Questions The Actor wonders: How were you expressing yourself when you felt most happy? Were you talking? Were you silent? Were you teaching? Were you learning? Were you serving? What were you doing or saying?

The Dancer's Life Purpose Questions The Dancer wonders: How were you feeling? Were you ecstatic? Were you peaceful? Were you enjoying solitude? Were you appreciating community? What was your main feeling? Which circumstances was that feeling connected to?

The Critic's Life Purpose Questions The Critic wonders: Why was that time so perfect? What made it just right? Was it the exquisite environment? Was it your fabulous choice of thoughts? Was it someone's admirable actions? Was it a perfect mood? What was done so well that it filled you so?

The Score Composer's Life Purpose Questions The Score Composer wonders: What was it all about? What deep dream did your happiness express? What ancient wish did it fulfill? Have you experienced that dream in other forms throughout your life? What forms? If you summed up the basic dream or wish in one or two words, what words would they be? Is it a universal wish with a personal dream describing it?

The Set Designer's Life Purpose Questions The Set Designer wonders: What kind of environment were you in? What were the conditions of that environment? What was well taken care of in that environment?

The Stage Manager's Life Purpose Questions The Stage Manager wonders: Whom did you benefit? How did you benefit them? What was their response?

The Playwright's Life Purpose Questions The Playwright wonders: What story did you tell yourself about the event? What happened?

The Director's Life Purpose Questions The Director wonders: How did each of the others affect you? What caused your happiness in relationship to everyone involved?

The Lighting Designer's Life Purpose Questions The Lighting Designer wonders: Where did you place your focus? How did your focus contribute to the enjoyment you experienced at that time in your life?

The Sound Designer's Life Purpose Questions The Sound Designer wonders: What was your contribution to the mood of the situation? What were you feeling deep within?

The Promoter's Life Purpose Questions The Promoter wonders: What was the best part of whatever happened? What is unique about your story? What part of the story is inspiring to you? What happened that woke you up and moved you? What changed your mood, perception, or life? Whatever inspired you will inspire others when shared in a story.

The Audience's Life Purpose Questions The Audience Member wonders: What was it that allowed you to accept yourself so deeply in that situation? What did you witness and allow without judgment?

■ ■ ■

Think upon these things in silence or write them down. You may choose to share your answers with a significant other or friend. You may wish to explore your answers further with a chosen art form.

By contemplating these questions, you will discover that all circumstances surrounding your happiness were simply the form in which your happiness arrived. When I was a theater director I was very happy during performances, but it wasn't theater that truly made me happy. Bringing people together in a celebration of love and expression brought me joy because I brought my joy to the act.

You bring happiness to life, and life mirrors it right back. Then you think that life has graced you with joy today but life may not be so kind tomorrow. You are actually the initial channel of that joy. As long as you give joy to life, it will give it back to you. Living in a state of joy is an opportunity that is available to you all the time. Life is your mirror.

You become what you focus on. Life offers every feeling, quality, mood, and thought you can imagine twenty-four hours a day. You pick which aspect of life you choose to view. Whatever you are, you see in others. Life plus you is simply a two-way mirror and choice is the act of focusing the lens on a particular aspect of life. You can choose misery, and you can choose ecstasy.

The situation surrounding your happiness is the vehicle. There is a central reason for your happiness that you found in that vehicle. For some it is adventure, for others service, for others peace, and for others expression.

Once you identify the central source of your deepest happiness, you can be happy anywhere. For example, if your primary source of happiness is communion, you can commune with someone wherever you are. You can commune with people, animals, nature, and Spirit. If you identify the primary source of your happiness to be good feelings in your body, take care of your body, and you will have good feelings wherever you are. If you find the central source of your happiness comes from expressing yourself, do so wherever you are and you will be happy.

Live in Response to Your Essential Purpose and Let Life Provide the Details

Your central source of happiness is your purpose. It is offered to you abundantly because you know how to create it. Thus, you have an endless supply to share with others. When you create a career that is based on your central source of happiness, your happiness can multiply all over the planet. When you give to others, all the joy that your receivers feel is also felt by you.

A year and a half after I gave up my theater troupe to go to graduate school, I was in a state of despair. I called John, an old buddy from high school. I told him that I had made a mistake and wasn't sure if I could pull the pieces together.

"Pull the pieces together?" he said. "You don't even understand what you're doing yet. You think this is all about a theater troupe. You have to get clear about your purpose and who you are. You're a person who knows how to love life and love yourself, Laurie, and you were that long before your theater troupe. You see the shining light in others. That's your gift. You don't need the troupe to give to humanity what you are here to give. You have to let go of the form. There's another form and it isn't completely up to you as to what it is. Concentrate on your purpose, and you'll do what you are here to do." His words surprised me, and I let them sink into my heart where they have lived for years.

I also spoke to my closest girlfriend. She said, "Laurie, your work has always been to teach people how to love who they truly are. It's not the theater troupe."

Four years later, I was giving Creative Intimacy seminars, feeling happier and more on purpose than ever before, and giving a gift that allows others to deeply change their lives. My purpose is not the theater troupe nor is it the workshop. My purpose is to be Playwright and a Director, creating positive perspective and bringing others into states of love. When I honor this I am delighted with living.

In simple terms my purpose is to be happy. Being happy to me means being creatively expressive and serving others in the process. My purpose is to shine my light on others so that their lights shine. Everyone is shining light, and when you carry out your deepest heart-felt purpose, you can feel this. When you choose to do something of service that makes you very happy, you can be emotionally, lovingly, spiritually, and financially fulfilled. You have abundant love to give.

Know and honor yourself. You don't have complete control over who you are. Your talents and personality traits are gifts from life to you. You can resist them and be unhappy. But why do that when you can love them, use them, cherish them, and be a joyous servant to life!

The voice of life is made of love, whether it is sunny and summer or bitter cold and winter. He is the lighter of campfire in your heart, the pansy garden rainwater wine, the human muscle of a mountain walk, the rise of muffin bedded in baking tin. The voice of life takes on many forms and shapes and so do you. Celebrate the unfolding mystery of yourself!

6 · Creative Support

Clarifying and Communicating What You Need

Knowing who you are and what you need from yourself makes it possible for you to live a fulfilling life and attract wonderful circumstances more often. Responding to your own needs and knowing your purpose do not guarantee, however, that others will always know what you desire from them. It is your job to clarify and communicate to others what it is that you desire from them. This way, you will feel supported and loved. When you ask, you will find that people love to give. When you ask and someone says no, the matter is immediately clear and you can turn to someone else for support. It is important to respect another person's choice to say no without incurring bad feelings.

Jeanette was distraught because she wanted more love from Paul. Paul was disappointed because he deeply loved Jeanette, showed her his love every day, and never got the appreciation he craved. After months of anguish, they came to a coaching session and discovered that Jeanette wanted more verbal appreciation and Paul wanted more help around the house.

Paul had assumed that everything he did around the house and his physical affection were what Jeanette wanted when she said she wanted more love. What Jeanette actually desired were more compliments and verbally expressed adoration. She assumed Paul knew this but she hadn't told him directly.

Jeanette also assumed that Paul meant he wanted her to give him more compliments when he said he wanted appreciation. She had purposefully done this and couldn't understand the reason for his being upset with her. He hadn't ever clarified that he wanted her to help out when he did something to improve their home. In his eyes, her helping out would be a way of showing that she valued what he was doing. He thought she knew this.

Neither had understood each other. Jeanette guessed inaccurately that Paul wanted what she wanted. Paul guessed incorrectly that Jeanette wanted what he wanted. When they took a moment to clarify, the solution became obvious and simple. Jeanette helped out more around the house, and Paul verbally expressed his love.

When you are disappointed that you are not getting from others what you need, you must address the issue in a clearer way. If you want a particular type of support, you must identify it and ask for it.

You must be very specific with your request. Sometimes your partner will sense what you need. This is a precious experience. However, you cannot make your partner into a twenty-four-hour-a-day mind reader. A gift asked for and received is just as valuable as a surprise. It is evidence of your partner's devotion to you.

Assume directorship of your life and live in a blame-free learning arena: the life play. Be clear about what you desire. Only you know what that is, how you want it, when you want it, where you want it, how often you want it, and how much of it you want. It is easy to blame your partner for not giving you what you want without knowing what that is yourself. Take time to clarify.

Be flexible with what you are here to give. When someone asks something of you that causes you to stretch, you are being given an opportunity to expand your generosity and compassion, and thus your happiness. I asked my boyfriend to touch me in a certain way, and doing so brought him great joy. Another time, I asked him to focus on what he was grateful for immediately after I heard him complain about our relationship, and doing so brought him more happiness.

Know and say what you want, and watch your relationships improve significantly. My boyfriend asked me to accept his need for time alone, and accepting him gave me inner strength. He asked me to be more communicative about my needs, and when I realized I had the capacity to do so, I became more self-confident. Our partner's challenges and requests are opportunities for more delight than we have ever imagined. Stay attached to old modes of being and watch your frustration mount. Surrender to requests of love and wonderful surprises will be yours.

Choose to remain in love with your partner, your life, your body, your sexuality, your spirituality, your career, and your money. (Money is simply a form of energy which you can turn into something good or something stressful via your attitude. Why not turn all of life into the energy of love?) When you feel tense or challenged, choose love. Would you rather be in love or in frustration? It's a choice. Would you like to be a person who can only be in love under very particular circumstances? Such a person is a cast character, a victim of life. Put love first and joy shall spring forth eternally.

To Be a Person Who Receives Support Do the Following:

- Specifically identify what you want.
- Get even more specific.
- Ask for what you desire.
- If your partner or the person you are turning to with a request says no, find another way to respond to your own need. Ask someone else or be creative.
- If your usual way of asking creates upset, try asking in another way.
- Be flexible with how you receive support and you will begin to recognize that support is coming to you in many ways consistently.
- Regardless of the fleeting circumstances, choose to stay in love. Your only choice is to be in love with life or not to be. Is there really a better option than to be in love with life?

■ ■ ■

You can easily mistake the desire for a qualitative experience with the desire for a particular circumstance. For example, someone might believe that he is upset about his lack of money, when truly he craves security or freedom. Some millionaires believe they don't have enough, while other people live in financial poverty but experience profound security. Often your despair comes from focusing on a particular idea about what you believe you need rather than identifying your deepest needs. People will help you when they are clear about the essential core of your wishes.

When I was twenty, I had a peak revelation during which I remembered that I came into this life to learn unconditional love. Everything else was simply a tool to do this. I decided that I would create a theater troupe whose purpose was to express authentic love of the genuine self.

I became consumed with the desire to succeed, however, and soon forgot my purpose. Every theater troupe I designed fell apart after interpersonal conflict took over. At age twenty-six, I threw my hands in the air and said, "Spirit, obviously my purpose is not to create a theater troupe. I give up, so lead me to my purpose, Life!"

Within three days, I had created a theater troupe that changed people's lives, made the front page of the local newspaper, and was a great success. The theater troupe I had longed for arrived when I gave up. My personality type is Director, but when I made it my purpose rather than the tool for putting my purpose into service, nothing worked out.

After my first success I was full of gratitude, but soon my gratitude became unbalanced pride. I was more concerned with my success than with learning to give unconditional love and learning to create an environment in which people could unconditionally love. I thought that I had mastered my purpose and I deserved recognition and respect. My lack of humility took me off purpose, and I unconsciously set the stage for another apparent failure. When it came time to put on the second production, everyone who had been full of enthusiasm and devotion to the theater process ten months before quit.

I remember that day very well. I had horrible cramps, the air was sticky hot, and mosquitoes were everywhere. I went to meditate in a little tent by myself in the woods. During that meditation my heart spilled over with sorrow that turned back into love. I remembered my purpose and asked Spirit to keep my heart on track and let me serve humanity. Soon after my meditation, ten kids who decided that they wanted to be the new theater troupe approached me.

Years later when I started the Creative Intimacy workshops because I wanted to serve humanity and facilitate an environment in which people could learn to live in a state of love and miraculous communication, I forgot my purpose again. I became very concerned with my success and money. I forgot that my Director personality was a gift from Spirit so that I could serve humanity. I made myself the focus of my life rather than everyone around me. The workshops had started with a burst of success but slowed down into apparent failure with my change of heart.

One day at the peak of frustration, I asked Spirit for clarity in a meditation. As soon as I did, I remembered that my purpose was to give and receive unconditional love and to create a process which would allow others to do the same. As soon as I remembered my true purpose, I became happier than ever in my career, and my clients began to prosper in leaps and bounds. Success now occurred in terms of publicity, praise, money, and numbers, but it was no longer my focus. What mattered most was touching the hearts of others so that their lives could unfold in the arms of love and fulfillment.

Once you clarify your overall purpose in life, you will be able to clarify your purpose in any relationship a lot more easily. You will be more inclined to choose relationships that support you.

When you get clear about your purpose for being in a relationship, you will attract situations that serve you. People have different purposes for being in particular relationships at different times. Some people are in a relationship to share pleasure. Some are in a relationship to build self-esteem. Some are in a relationship to be loved. Some are in a relationship to mutually recover from old hurts. Some people are in relationships to learn something. Most of us have many reasons for being in relationships. Usually there are a couple of fundamental purposes in each specific relationship, which can be clarified by using the unique perspectives of each Creative Personality Type.

I had many unsolvable struggles with relationships until I clarified my primary purpose, which is mutual unconditional love and understanding, mutual unconditional inspiration and nourishment, and mutual unconditional support and respect. In sum, my relationship purpose is unconditional loving partnership. This occurs when two people are being themselves, sharing aligned purposes, and communicating clearly.

If you have not yet chosen your life partner, you will get a clearer perspective of what you seek by answering a question from each of the twelve personality types.

The Actor Helps Clarify Your Relationship Needs

The Actor asks, "What type of attention do you most like: someone who compliments you, someone who listens to you, someone who touches you, someone who watches you, someone who analyzes you, etc.?" Figure out what type of attention feeds you the most. It is mandatory that you pick a mate who easily and happily gives this type of attention.

The Dancer Helps Clarify Your Relationship Needs

The Dancer asks, "How do you like to feel? Is a good day passionate, peaceful, or a combination of both? Are you happy when your mate excites you or happier when he gives you a lot of solitude? Are you happier with a mate who provides a lot of comfort or with a mate who provides a lot of enthusiasm?" Think about the emotional environment that feeds you the most deeply. You are best off choosing a mate who easily co-creates such an environment.

The Critic Helps Clarify Your Relationship Needs

The Critic asks, "What is unacceptable in a mate? What is most important?" Make sure that the mate you choose does not have any unacceptable traits and gets an A grade on whatever is most important to you.

The Score Composer Helps Clarify Your Relationship Needs

The Score Composer asks, "What do you really want if anything is possible? Someone who cooks with you, someone who offers consistent compassion, someone who goes for walks with you every day, someone whose touch leaves you feeling euphoric, someone whose words tingle through your spine each time he or she speaks?" Tell the truth. Imagine you live in a blissed-out world where you get whatever you desire.

Your partner should keep you in touch with your deepest, most unrealistic dream at all times and fulfill this dream desire in you simultaneously. My boyfriend said, "When I met you and heard you laugh, your laugh awakened a deep longing in me and filled it in the same second. I fell in love." We choose partners because they answer a mysterious call inside us.

The Set Designer Helps Clarify Your Relationship Needs

The Set Designer asks, "What kind of environment do you like? Do you prefer a pastel interior in the bedroom? Do you keep your car clean? Is your house full of plants?" Choose a partner whose environment turns you on. It's essential to a happy co-existence.

The Stage Manager Helps Clarify Your Relationship Needs

The Stage Manager asks, "What do you want to contribute to a relationship? What do you want to give?" It is imperative that you choose a partner who is nourished and enlivened by your gifts.

The Playwright Helps Clarify Your Relationship Needs

The Playwright asks, "What type of life story are you here to write? Are you focused on a story of learning or is your preferred life story one of easygoing fun? What type of life story writing do you seek in a mate? Do you value a mate who is making her life into a challenging adventure, a peaceful and steady stroll, an upward hill of success? Do you wish to co-create a life story of unrelenting joy or do you want someone to agree with you on days that you feel life is disappointing?" Make sure that your partner's outlook on life is one that contributes to you and matches your values.

The Director Helps Clarify Your Relationship Needs

The Director says, "Your only happiness is shared happiness." If both of you feel great together, you are in the right situation. If not, see what you can do to improve the situation. If you can't improve things in the context of a one-year courtship, move on.

The Lighting Designer Helps Clarify Your Relationship Needs

The Lighting Designer says that you will do best by focusing on what you like and delight in. Fifty percent of our happiness in relationship comes from choosing an appropriate partner, but the other fifty percent comes from what we bring to our situation. Pay attention to what it is that you are choosing to focus upon if you desire happiness.

The Sound Designer Helps Clarify Your Relationship Needs

The Sound Designer asks, "What kind of unexplainable feelings do you have when your partner is with you? What is your internal mood?" Pay close attention to these feelings. They are as important as what is said and done. However, don't expect your feelings to be better with your partner than with yourself. Hormonal honeymoons will come to an end. If your partner can offer as many good feelings to you as you can offer to yourself, you will be in good shape.

The Promoter Helps Clarify Your Relationship Needs

The Promoter says, "Make sure that special, positive, memorable events are happening." If they are, you can live long and well together. Remember to talk about your joys and pick a mate who does the same. This will carry you a long way.

The Audience Member Helps Clarify Your Relationship Needs

The Audience Member says, "Observe. Whatever happens has value when we watch through the eyes of acceptance. All relationships serve a purpose."

■ ■ ■

Remember, the questions listed above can also be used to help clarify your desired career, spiritual existence, financial situation, ideal home, or sex life.

When Life or Another Disappoints You...
- Point yourself back in the right direction by remembering your essential purpose.
- Use the Creative Personality Types' unique form of wisdom to remember your essential purpose.

Still Stuck? Not Getting Your Needs Met by Others?
Often many of our needs will be met easily by others once we have explained them. However, when you have asked in every way you know how, and still nobody is giving to you in the way you desire, then you need to look back at yourself. Life is telling you that what you seek is mastery of a quality. You are looking for something outside because you cannot create it inside.

Before You Assume that Others are the Cause of Your Suffering, Assume that Life Has Surrounded You With a 360-Degree Mirror
I remember sitting in my apartment and looking at the silhouettes of trees splashed along the white wooden fence. As the sun dropped, the pictures changed. I thought to myself that the trees seemed fine regardless of how the projected images changed with the moving sun. A feeling of peace filled my abdomen and heart. Simultaneously, I felt very alone.

Movies and books often portray loneliness as a feeling of lack, but I felt quite at peace in my loneliness. It felt like a part of life, just like communion with close ones is an ongoing part of life. I meditated a while. Soon I felt a desire to connect with others, so I called friends on the phone. I simply wanted to share my experience.

Each friend I called responded with opinions and judgments about my loneliness. Someone had suggestions about what I should do. Another person offered reasons for why I felt lonely. Someone else listed causes and others to blame for my condition. I became increasingly frustrated. My loneliness was simply a feeling. All I wanted was to be witnessed and accepted in the reality of my human loneliness.

I called my boyfriend and told him that I simply wanted to be understood and witnessed. He didn't understand this. He repeatedly asked me to tell him what kind of insights I was getting about life from my experience of peaceful loneliness. By this point I was not at all at peace with my loneliness. I was exasperated.

There must be a way to be together without having to evaluate each other's experiences, I thought to myself. I called another friend and tried to explain my experience. She praised me for being "enlightened."

"I just want to be witnessed," I said. "I'm not enlightened. I'm not messed up. I just am."

"How Buddha-like," she replied, "Have you been studying Buddhism?" I hadn't been and felt misheard again.

At last I realized I was in a fight with myself. I wanted everyone to accept me for who I was; yet I was evaluating each of them for being who they were. I let their opinions slide off my heart. I appreciated the warmth of friends as I made a few more calls. My frustration with opinions and criticisms was my battle, so I decided to accept each person in the way that I wanted to be accepted, simply received and seen.

It was now clear that my exasperation and others' critiques were one and the same. Both were simply acts of individuation and self-preservation. Subtly costumed yet deeply alive in the universal psyche is a shared fear that something precious can be taken away from us by others, but truly all we have to lose is love, peace, the ability to receive, and the willingness to give. Nobody takes this from us. We lose it by failing to practice it.

I wanted to remain peaceful, yet I was inviting others' responses to motivate me into a state of anger. The only way back to peace was to offer to others what I had wanted them to give: an ear that listens without knowing what is best for anyone at any time. I practiced being a source of support without concern as to who was good or bad, right or wrong, better or worse. When I provided the acceptance for others that I desired to experience, I found peace. I no longer needed others to create acceptance for me. Miraculously, when I was the source of acceptance, it was mirrored back to me.

After I made this internal shift, my boyfriend became very good at simply listening to and understanding what I was going through. He became one of my best listeners, which gave me a lot of room to grow with loving support. Changing your internal treatment of yourself does not guarantee that another will change in a particular way. However, I have witnessed time and time again that when I make an internal change or a client or friend makes an internal change, new characters show up in our lives to affirm the change or old characters suddenly change their roles.

I asked Spirit to be with me and immediately she was. Everything I had wanted from the outside, I had from the inside. We co-create with Spirit every day. We co-create with our gratitude as well as our complaints. We speak to the unknown in the supposed privacy of our mind and in doing so, we co-create a web of thoughts and actions. We attract people to us who agree with our viewpoints and resonate with our energetic stance, and then we make worlds with our mutual mental viewpoints and energetic patterns.

It is okay and sometimes necessary to speak to Spirit in all kinds of ways. We can thank Spirit, give to Spirit, ask of Spirit and even demand cooperation from Spirit. If we only plead to Spirit, we become disempowered in our life directorship and give authority to something outside ourselves. Yet when we take complete authority and co-operate with Spirit, we become the quality that we are looking for. Most of the time we are seeking life qualities. We say we want money, outcomes, and situations but it is the fulfillment derived from the money, outcomes, and situations, that we truly seek. The kinder, more loving, and generous we become, the happier we are. Feeling supported is actually the combination of receiving and giving.

Assume that Spirit wants something for you. If you are blaming, frustrated, judging others, uncomfortable, or trying to hide from yourself then you have not identified and accepted what it is that Spirit is asking of your personality. Learn to embrace and become your highest self now. If you wait you will suffer and still have to undergo the needed transformation. Face it while you can do something about it, and you will feel pleasure and fulfillment. Rise to the occasion of your highest self by becoming what you seek, and you will live with passion yet simultaneous peace.

I remember meeting an elderly woman named Jilian. Her essence seemed bright like zinnias but her personality had become stiff and dry. From the light in her eyes, I sensed a powerful woman living within a held-back demeanor. She was very isolated. She used to wake up at 4 AM to put on make-up and get dressed. She rarely spoke to the other women in the nursing home. She walked into the living room one morning, trying to contain herself in a tightly buttoned little dress over a girdle. She spilled into the living room, knocking over a vase of flowers. Water saturated the dusty rug. Flowers decorated the room. Another woman's laugh made the music.

"Excuse me," she said awkwardly as if trying to dry the rug with her words. Her verbal language was too tight for her inner feelings, and unfinished stories came falling into the living room for other women to hear. Her tears dripped, then dashed. Her little sighs, which had marked her presence in the home, were too tiny for her oceanly emotions and that day she gushed.

Some of the staff thought that she fell apart right then, but I am sure she came alive. The more she cried, the more she shone. Stories of disappointment expressed, softened into stories of gratitude. Her rocky words tumbled in her tears until they became polished and smooth. She had waited many years to speak her truth and be herself.

After that day she abandoned the girdle and became talkative and friendly. She left her isolation behind. This was a beautiful transformation to watch but also sad because of all the years she had contained herself and could have been happier. Because Jilian didn't clarify what she needed, it became clarified for her. She needed to share and be heard. Clarify your needs now so that you can have them fulfilled. Don't waste years in anger or frustration when knowing what you need can lead you to a life of joy and delight.

You can't escape from who you are, so know who you are well. If you zip up your desires, some day the sadness of ignoring them will take you over. If you blame others for not understanding you when you are not being clear, your anger will grow like fungus. If you honor and communicate your desires, becoming both the giver and the receiver, you will be danced through life like a maple tree's seed pods joyously settling on the ground of who you truly are.

7 · Creative Spirituality

How You Speak With Life

If you have tried out exercises from preceding chapters, you are probably realizing that you are a very powerful Director in your own life. Although circumstances beyond your control have occurred regularly, how you have responded to those circumstances has been your choice. Each situation that life provides has invited you to choose between love or fear in one way or another.

When you make the choice to behave from a loving existence, you bring out the best in those around you. When you make the choice to act from a place of fear, you inspire others' fear. Remember that love and fear can both take on a variety of forms, as explained in Chapter Three. Love can appear as many qualities, including generosity, compassion, and gratitude. Fear can appear as anger, jealousy, and destructive criticism, among many other traits.

In the same way that we create our relationships with other people, we create an ongoing relationship with Spirit. Whether you know Spirit as Spirit, a Messiah who has not yet arrived, Adonai, Jesus, Buddha, Allah, Krishna, all of life, the one within all, Divine Mother, your ancestors, or someone else, you have a relationship with that entity. If you are an atheist, you have a relationship with life in general, so you also will be able to utilize the information in this chapter while continuing to honor your beliefs. You co-create your relationship with Spirit or life with your thoughts, actions, words, and feelings.

If you are not happy with your relationship with Spirit or life, it is likely that you are also not happy with your relationship with yourself and those around you. Gratitude and responsibility are keys to creating a happy relationship with Spirit and life. By focusing on what you are thankful for and taking responsibility for what disturbs you, you situate yourself in an empowered place. As long as you have gratitude, you will have joy. As long as you hold yourself responsible for the role you play in any particular situation, you are free to co-create change as you see fit.

The Key to Satisfaction
- Be thankful for all the gifts life gives you.
- Take a Director role and create what you seek.

■ ■ ■

For many years I felt that something was missing in my life. I was never quite where I wanted to be. Although I was very in love with my boyfriend, he wasn't exactly what I wanted for a lifetime partner. Although I had many fascinating and kind friends, most of them didn't live up to my expectations. Financially, I wasn't making what I desired. I questioned if I had chosen the right town in which to live. I endlessly fantasized about the perfect life, the best mate, the right friends, and a miraculous town.

At some point in my search, I realized that all of my problems were essentially the same. I believed I wasn't getting what I most wanted. I had been speaking to Spirit and life from a viewpoint of lack. I realized that my viewpoint was my only problem. Instead of trying to switch my boyfriend, my town, my friends, and my finances, I decided to switch my relationship with Spirit and life. Instead of subtly suggesting to Spirit that nothing was enough, I decided to look at my life from a viewpoint of abundance.

I practiced treasuring all that I had, all those that I knew, and all the gifts that life was giving to me. In doing this, the gifts multiplied and so did my feeling of satisfaction with my boyfriend, my friends, my town, my finances, myself, and Spirit. I felt that Spirit was completely on my side.

When you give life fear, life gives fear right back. Substitute that fear point of view with a love point of view. When you give love to Spirit and life, it comes back to you immediately. You can feel it, see it, taste it, and hear it.

In order to change your problems with Spirit or life in an everlasting way, you must identify them from the outside. Instead of perceiving yourself to be a character cast in a play you did not write, assume that you are the Director and you are choosing your role. Look carefully at your role.

You must look below the surface. Forget about the details, the names, the events, and look for the essential issue of fear that you are giving to life. You can express things that ail you through journaling, talking, contemplating, or any art form. Once you put the problem into art you look at it, ask questions, and imagine it answering you. You can use the chart in Chapter Three to assist you in this process.

Jennifer was very upset because none of her relationships had worked out long term. She felt unable to try again. She was angry at Spirit. She decided to draw a spontaneous picture about her problem. Her self-portrait was of a woman who was slouched over and had given up. The unplanned self-portrait, drawn by following her impulses, appeared drastically different from this woman who had a straight athlete's back and held her head high, the image she ordinarily carried.

She looked at the picture and asked, "What's the matter?" Although it may sound funny to hear that a woman was talking to her drawing, it was her way of loosening up her defenses and allowing her unconscious mind to speak. When we are playful and creative, we often get to the truth of our own matters very quickly.

Immediately, these words came to her: "I can't work any more. I've worked and worked at relationships and I'm tired. Choose a man who doesn't make me work so hard."

"How?" She dialogued with this newly revealed part of herself. "All of the men I like are complex and challenging."

"It's simple," her unconscious mind said, "Find a mate with whom you can easily laugh and play and share a similar lifestyle. If you like challenge, share the challenge of making life together better and better."

After taking a long brisk walk, Jennifer wrote a story about the new kind of relationship she desired. The more she wrote, the more her fantasy seemed possible. She began to feel thankful to life for bringing her new realizations. As she focused on her gratitude, she found that she also was thankful for ways in which previous boyfriends had contributed to her.

Now she was able to relax, release the ongoing struggle, and enjoy life. Instead of relating to Spirit with an attitude of struggle based on a fear of never getting what she wanted, she offered her joyfulness. In doing so she felt grateful for life and happy. In this mode, she began to attract more easygoing men. Her unconscious mind had known what was troubling her all along. By expressing it through art, Jennifer was able to see it clearly and change it.

The next man that she dated was very much like the fellow she had creatively imagined and written about. The relationship was very different and far more satisfying than previous ones. Her conversations with Spirit had become full of love and thanks, and her relationship mirrored this.

After identifying the role that she was playing, Jennifer clarified what it was that she really sought and chose a new role that matched her quest. Instead of blaming Spirit for what wasn't working, she took responsibility for herself and thanked Spirit for all the ways Spirit had contributed to her.

Jennifer expressed the part of herself that she wanted to discontinue inhabiting. Find a creative way to do this yourself. Use art, talking, or writing. Ask that part of you what it wants and needs. Ironically, you can't eliminate a part of yourself by trying to excise it. You must find out what it yearns for. A part that is acting out in some way is calling for what you need the most.

Like Jennifer, utilize your breath and body. The intellect is not enough to make a profound and lasting change. Do something physical that brings your awareness into your breathing and body, and you will access an ability to change much more easily.

Jennifer's process led her naturally to change her conversation with Spirit about relationship, and consequently attract a good mate for her. Sometimes you will need to take an active role in redesigning your approach to communicating with Spirit. Note the conversations you are having with Spirit in your area of difficulty. If they no longer serve you, choose new conversations. Find new ways to relate to Spirit and life that come from a positive, loving place.

You are talking to Spirit or life all day regardless of what you are doing. Whether you are communicating with a beloved, giving instructions to a colleague, cleaning the porch, or paying the credit card bill, you are talking to Spirit. You are making life beautiful or ugly, warm or cold, sweet or sour every moment.

When you notice that there is an area of life in which you cannot easily operate from a positive stance, you have the opportunity to be curious about why, and to make a change. The answer to why always involves the role in which you have cast yourself in your current life scene. Remember that you are the Director, so you send out the callback invitations whenever you wish.

Significant Steps for Changing Your Relationship With Spirit

- Be aware of the role you are playing in your life that is causing you to suffer.
- Using art, meditations, or your mind, choose to change that role.
- Be aware of the thought-conversations you have with Spirit in regard to an area of life with which you are not satisfied.
- Change the thought-conversations so that they are positive and full of gratitude.
- Notice the changes that begin to occur in your real life.

■ ■ ■

Everyone has personal areas of existence that can be revised to better serve the goal of happiness because imperfection is the nature of being human. It is often in areas of struggle that you discover your greatest assets and strengths. View your areas of hardship with gratitude, for they are your best teachers and can lead you to abundant treasures. My shyness taught me to be compassionate, bold, grateful, and deeply accepting. The rewards it led me to far outweigh the pain it caused me in the long run.

Each of the twelve Creative Personality Types is wisest about a particular domain of living. By examining your conversations with Spirit and life within each of these areas and utilizing the suggested steps, you can create very positive changes and results. Those who are not satisfied in a particular area of existence can find deepening satisfaction, while those who are experiencing adequacy will have the opportunity to create ecstasy.

Personality Types and Chakras

Review the following life areas and choose which ones you want to work with. You may want to work with all of them over time.

While some people benefit most from approaching these areas conceptually, others who are somatically oriented will approach this exercise in a body-centered fashion. Each of the Creative Personality Types' Domain has a corresponding center of energy located in the body. These energy centers are known as chakras. You can physically or energetically focus on a body center, to discover any obstacles in your way of living to the fullest. Once you are aware of an obstacle, you can release it, and give birth to a new and constructive force. By addressing chakra weakness, you can improve your relationship to the corresponding domain.

The Actor's Chakra

The Actor personality is primarily concerned with the power of the self and authentic expression. The Actor expresses emotions and strength of self in the world. If your relationship with Spirit is positive in this area of your life, you are accustomed to feeling satisfied in your relationship to others and the world. You feel that your role in the world is good, adequately expressed, and sufficiently recognized. Your emotions are familiar and comfortable to you, integrated into your self-expression in a powerful way. Your expression is valuable to others in your experience.

If your relationship to Spirit encompasses fear in this area of life, you are having trouble truly expressing who you are, showing your emotions with a savvy acceptance of your personality, and reaching your fullest potential for sharing yourself in the world. You believe that you are not adequately known by others. You are experiencing a sense of not being good enough, which leads to communication difficulties such as power struggles, victimhood, and cruelty to others.

The Actor's chakra is the solar plexus. You can feel this area beginning a couple of inches below your belly and extending up to your heart.

Exercise: Developing Your Actor's Chakra Try this exercise every day for two weeks. Express yourself in a situation in which remaining silent would be easier. Keep a journal of how you felt immediately after doing this as well as six hours later.

The Dancer's Chakra

The Dancer's area is that of passion and creation, including sexuality, and generation. This applies to relationship and family as well as to any creative act in life. Whether you are having a baby or giving birth to a business, you draw on the powers of passion and creation.

If you are happy with the degree of passion in your life, sexually fulfilled, and creatively consummated, then your relationship to Spirit and life in the area of passion is healthy. You feel that you flow through life with inspiration.

If life is dull, if you find your passion for living is stagnant, if you feel sexually incomplete, you will benefit from revising your relationship to Spirit in the chakra of passion.

The chakra associated with the Dancer is the sexual chakra. This chakra is centered around the vagina in women and the penis in men.

Exercise: Developing Your Dancer's Chakra Try this exercise every day for two weeks. Each morning before getting out of bed, keep your eyes closed and do a body survey. Breathe deep into your belly and up into your chest, placing your awareness on your toes, noticing any physical sensations, and moving your toes in any way that feels good by following all impulses.

Repeat this process with each of your body parts: feet, ankles, calves, knees, thighs, hips, genitals, buttocks, back, stomach, chest, shoulders, arms, elbows, palms, fingers, neck, head, face, scalp.

Keep a journal on how you feel right after doing this, as well as six hours later.

The Critic's Chakra

The Critic's domain is the area of life in which we revise, refine, redesign, and develop. We take what has already been given and shape it into something better.

If you feel that projects, standards, and goals in your life are being met as well as possible, your relationship with Spirit in the redesigning domain is healthy. If you are effortlessly able to identify ways to make improvements, then you are doing well in this area of life.

If you find that projects or interactions are lacking, and mediocrity is your standard, you will benefit from reshaping your relationship with Spirit in the redesigning domain. When you know that you have settled for less but can't clarify what would make life better, you can improve your relationship to Critic's chakra.

The chakra connected to the Critic's domain is located in the palms of the hands.

Exercise: Developing Your Critic's Chakra Try doing this exercise every day for two weeks. At the end of the day choose a project in process, plan in the works, or situation that you participated in during the day. If you are addressing a situation, make a list of ways in which you could have improved the situation so that next time you will be better prepared to make a similar situation better. If you are addressing a project or plan, make a list of ways to improve the project or plan as you continue to carry it out.

The Score Composer's Chakra

The Score Composer's area of life is that of grace. The Score Composer opens herself to the gifts that life offers to us which are beyond our control. They are the gifts of personality and potential.

If you feel you can trust life and that things tend to work out in a way that is meaningful, you are in a healthy spiritual relationship with the grace domain of life. When you know your desires and dreams in simple and positive terms, your Score Composer's chakra is in a state of well-being and vitality.

If you find that your will is in overdrive, you can't ever relax and expect situations to happen by the grace of life and others' input, you will benefit from changing your relationship to

Spirit in the grace domain. If you are concerned with changing details and circumstances but never feel more content as a result of doing so, your relationship to grace needs adjusting. If your dreams at night are complicated, your thoughts in the day leave you feeling strained, and your desires are murky to you, then your grace chakra is not in a state of health.

The grace chakra is located on the crown of the head.

Exercise: Developing Your Score Composer's Chakra Practice this exercise once a week for one month. Do this exercise before falling asleep. If you fall asleep during the exercise that is also fine.

Find some music that allows your mind to drift and dream. Lie down on your bed and ask Spirit to guide you to your most precious and fulfilling dream. Turn on the music and let your mind and heart wander.

The Set Designer's Chakra

The Set Designer's area is that of practicality. The Set Designer is focused on making sure that the house has a strong foundation, meals are nurturing, and clothes are mended. The Set Designer carries out the physical actions that are necessary for a quality life.

If you feel well taken care of, nourished and warm, sure that your bills are paid, your relationship with the practical domain of life is healthy. If you can count on yourself to get things done in a way that feels good, then you are experiencing a vital relationship with the practical domain of life.

If you feel depleted, insecure about finances, undernourished, and not well-maintained, you will benefit from changing your relationship with the practical domain of life. If you can't count on yourself to get things done and feel that the practical aspects of your life are in disarray, it is time to improve your relationship to the practical necessities of living.

The Set Designer's domain is connected to the root chakra, which is located in the perineum.

Exercise: Developing Your Set Designer's Chakra Practice this exercise every day for two weeks. At the end of your day make a list of anything you procrastinated on. Make a commitment to take care of it at the earliest realistically possible time. Figure out when this time is and put it in your calendar. When the time arrives, write down any feelings or thoughts that are trying to convince you to procrastinate some more. Throw the list away and do what you committed to do.

The Stage Manager's Chakra

The Stage Manager's area of life is the domain of support. The Stage Manager makes sure there is enough acknowledgment, love, and assistance included in any endeavor. The Stage Manager has an ability to serve others.

If you are known to lend a helping hand and find that others are readily available to help you, then you have a healthy relationship with Spirit in the domain of support. If giving to others in need is a natural act for you and asking for others' support when you are in need is equally as comfortable, you have solid relationship to the domain of support.

If you find that you are hesitant to give your time or energy to the well-being of others and to encourage them in their endeavors, or if you rarely receive such support yourself, then you will benefit from modifying your relationship with Spirit in the realm of support.

The chakra associated with the Stage Manager is centered in the spine between the shoulders and extends into the upper back, shoulder, and base of the neck.

Exercise: Developing Your Stage Manager's Chakra Do this exercise every day for two weeks. Every other day find a way to lend a helping hand to another. Keep a journal about how it felt to do so. On the days you are not lending a hand, make it a point to ask someone to help or support you. Keep a journal about how it felt to do so.

The Playwright's Chakra

The Playwright's realm of expertise is the area of viewpoint. The Playwright takes what occurs and puts it into the stories that determine how we make sense of life's occurrences. The Playwright finds meaning in events whether they are joyful and effortless or challenging and painful.

If the stories you tell about your life and other people lead to positive meaning, then your relationship with Spirit in the viewpoint domain is healthy. If you describe the story of what life brings to you in a way that leaves you feeling grateful and lighthearted, you have a healthy relationship with the domain of viewpoint.

If you are constantly complaining to yourself and to others, you will benefit from refining your relationship to Spirit in the realm of viewpoint. If your challenges lead you to dire conclusions, your pain leads you to feeling like a victim, and the lessons you take from life are negative, you are suffering in the chakra of viewpoint. You will benefit by changing your relationship to this area of life.

The Playwright's chakra is located in an energy center six inches above the head.

Exercise: Developing Your Playwright's Chakra Practice this exercise once a week for one month. Choose a true story from your life which left you with unresolved feelings, pessimistic thoughts, or an experience of being victimized. Write an essay or make a list of ways in which that event invited you to grow. Look at what life may have been teaching you with that event when you do your writing. Think and write about the opportunity that event presented which invited you to become a fuller person.

The Lighting Designer's Chakra

The Lighting Designer's area of mastery is that of well-being. The Lighting Designer can shine light on goodness. The Lighting Designer focuses on the best parts of all situations.

If you feel that life is generally good regardless of circumstances, you have a healthy relationship with Spirit in the realm of well-being. If you smell the flowers rather than the trash, hear the compliment rather than the insult, and see the beauty rather than the imperfections, then your well-being chakra is healthy.

If you find that life throws you about—one day you are on top of a mountain, and the next you are in the depth of despair—you can benefit by developing your relationship to Spirit in the realm of well-being. If you are more concerned with the lemon seed that dropped in the soup than how delicious the soup tastes, then you will benefit by developing your relationship to the domain of well-being.

The Lighting Designer's chakra is located between the belly button and the top of the pubic hair.

Exercise: Developing Your Lighting Designer's Chakra Practice this exercise every day for two weeks. Fold a sheet of paper (or more if needed) in half length-wise. At the end of the day, make a list of all unfavorable experiences you encountered throughout the day on the left side of the paper. On the right side, directly across from each experience you listed, write down what you were focusing on when you had the unfavorable experience.

Turn your paper over. On the left side, for each of your experiences on the first list, write down what you could have focused on in order to have a positive experience. On the right side, write down what you imagine your corresponding experience would have been had you picked the positive focus.

The Director's Chakra

The Director's area is the domain of love. The Director knows that love is the result of people working well together and the

Director knows how to facilitate this. The Director brings the love out of everyone involved and feels overflowing with love in the process.

If you feel that there is always enough love for you and you always have enough love to give, then your relationship with Spirit in the realm of love is healthy. If your heart is full of love and you are attentive to your relationships with others, you are balanced in the domain of the Director. If you are good at including those around you, bringing people together, and making yourself a warm part of situations involving others, you are doing well in the domain of love.

If you are lacking love either as a receiver or giver, you will benefit by re-tuning your relationship to Spirit in the realm of love. If you feel alone, disengaged from others, or simply unaware of your connection with people around you, your Director's chakra can use some development.

The Director's domain is located in the heart.

Exercise: Developing Your Director's Chakra Practice this exercise once a week for a month. Choose a situation in which you felt disappointed. Write down what you think each person in the situation including yourself desired. Write down a way in which each person's desire could have been satisfied.

After doing your writing, sit quietly with your eyes closed and focus on your heart. Stay in a heart meditation for a minimum of ten minutes.

The Sound Designer's Chakra

The Sound Designer's arena of mastery is that of mood. The Sound Designer is skilled at bringing out the best in people by providing a mood that feels uplifting and inspired. The Sound Designer can become the leader at turning new ideas into reality with inspiration that is felt when words fall short. This is because the Sound Designer can touch your heart and bring out your best. Creating mood rather than waiting for mood to take over without a choice is the Sound Designer's forte.

If you are able to choose to be in a good mood, able to access meditative realms, able to feel ecstasy from within, then your relationship to the mood domain of life is highly developed.

If you are unable to call forth feelings of elation from inside yourself, you will benefit by changing your relationship to Spirit in the domain of mood. If you are in a battle with your own moods, feeling that they fall upon you like the rain and often wishing they were different, you will want to make your mood chakra healthier.

The Sound Designer's chakra is located in the feet where the human world and the natural world connect.

Exercise: Developing Your Sound Designer's Chakra Practice this exercise for one month. Pick a consistent thirty minutes that you can devote to this exercise on a daily basis.

Sit somewhere quietly where you will be undisturbed. Write down a one-word description of the mood you would like to experience. Make a list of everything you will need to let go of in order to experience that mood.

Sit in an upright, comfortable, seated position with your eyes closed. Ask Spirit to open your heart and fill it with your desired mood.

If you are unsuccessful imagine yourself letting go of whatever is in the way. Make up a visual image that represents you letting go of the undesired mood. Breathe deeply and sigh, releasing the unwanted feeling on the out breath. Massage your heart and let the unwanted mood go back into the ethers.

Repeat the meditation of asking Spirit to open your heart and fill it with your desired mood.

The Promoter's Chakra

The Promoter's area of expertise is the realm of communication. The Promoter knows how to reach out to others in a way that calls forth excitement and interest.

If you find that what you have to say generally has a positive effect on others, your relationship with Spirit in the realm of communication is healthy. If people want to be around you after you have spoken, your communication chakra is in a good state.

If your communication often leaves others upset or dissatisfied, then you will benefit by changing your relationship to Spirit in the realm of communication. If people avoid you once they have spoken to you, then there is work for you to do in the Promoter's chakra.

The Promoter's chakra is located in the throat.

Exercise: Developing Your Promoter's Chakra Practice this exercise every day for two weeks. Each day give a minimum of one person verbal encouragement. Keep a journal of how you felt immediately after giving the encouragement.

Choose one day in each of the two weeks to give yourself verbal encouragement. Look at yourself in the mirror and speak to yourself.

The Audience Member's Chakra

The Audience Member's expertise lies in the arena of wisdom. Wisdom is the ability to see things from a view that transcends your own personal agenda. Wisdom is the act of maintaining a respectful awareness of others' highest selves at all times.

For example, when Tina said to Kevin, "Let's just forget this relationship altogether," Kevin could have felt hurt and yelled back, "Fine, I don't care about it anyway."

Being a wise Audience Member, however, he was acutely aware of Tina's hurt feelings and asked, "What can I do to help you feel more loved?"

When treated kindly, Tina responded without anger. "I just need more acknowledgment. I need to hear more about what you like about me."

"I love you," Kevin said. "I love you every minute even when I forget to say so. From now on, I'll tell you what I like about you more often, and I'll start now by saying I think that you are one of the smartest people I have ever known." The Audience Member sees everyone and everything with an ability to acknowledge.

If you are able to see motives, feelings, and questions below the surface of conversations and actions, and beyond your own desires, and you respond from a desire for the best, you are relating to Spirit from a healthy place. If you participate with respect and honor towards others, and consistently keep their best interests in mind, your relationship to the domain of wisdom is clear.

If you are quick to react, blame, and get upset, you will benefit from revising your relationship to this domain. If you cannot see with compassion and are strained from sizing people up, you can develop more wisdom. If you are more concerned with fleeting remarks and appearances than the highest good of all, your wisdom is waiting to be developed.

The Audience Member's chakra is located in the third eye, between the eyes and slightly above the eyebrow.

Exercise: Developing Your Audience Member's Chakra Practice this exercise every day for two weeks. At the end of the day write down the name of someone you judged negatively. Take a guess about what he or she was desiring or needing when you were negatively judging. Write this down as well. Next, write down the thoughts you would have had about that person if your purpose had been to witness and support their highest potential.

■ ■ ■

When you feel in touch with your deepest and most healthy motives, you feel close to Spirit. When you can remove old wounds, non-constructive directions, and selfish, greedy, or dishonorable motives from your entire psyche, you can feel close to Spirit. You will notice that your desires and what happens are intimately connected, allowing you to feel good and contribute to others.

In order to make your intentions clear, while thinking about your life ask that you be fully in line with your highest potential. Breathe deeply after asking for this. Now ask that anything between you and your highest potential be removed.

One client had ongoing problems with finances. He was going to discontinue therapy because he had no incoming money and couldn't pay rent, so he decided to do an intention clearing to tune to prosperity. After making his intention clear, several unexpected opportunities to make money showed up in his life. Both he and his girlfriend were elated.

Another client suffered from feeling isolated and alone despite having a number of loving friends. After participating in the intention-clearing exercise he realized that self-gratitude was the missing ingredient in his life, and he found a new peacefulness by appreciating himself more. Another client was lacking fun and playfulness. After doing this exercise, he stopped searching for fun things to do and brought fun and playfulness to his family.

Another woman did this exercise because she repeatedly felt unsure and unsafe in the world. She was able to change her feeling of discomfort to a feeling of heart warmth and security. When we can't accomplish our goals or find happiness in our relationship, it is valuable to become aware of the parts of ourselves that are not clearly directed and to take personal responsibility in order to get back on our best track. Creating a conversation of positivity, constructiveness, and gratitude with Spirit is very valuable if you want to live a positive, constructive, and fulfilling life.

With no one standing by a lake, only the trees' shadows appear in the water's ripples. Once you arrive, the ripples become colored by the shades of your clothes, the shape of your smile, or the shape of your frown. The air, full of the subtle scent of pine forest and blackberry bush, changes when you enter the scene. Your perfume and your sweat flavor the air. Life is still by the pond, but when you make your entrance, emotions and thoughts are added to the scene. So it is with all of life. Spirit keeps breathing in and out. It is you who chooses the flavor, the attitude, and the conversation you have with life. Choose well, for the basis of your contentment is the experience you create. All other factors are secondary.

8 · Creative Decision-Making

Involving Different Parts of Your Personality in a Decision

Decision-making can be very challenging. In this chapter, we take a look at the many factors involved in making a good decision. Identifying your primary commitment in a decision will determine how you experience the results of the decision. Furthermore, this chapter will use the Creative Personality Types' areas of interest to guide you through a solid decision-making process. You will learn that consulting your inner baby, child, teenager, and adult can point you toward a durable decision. You will be given the seven significant areas to look at when making a decision. This chapter also addresses leaving or staying with a partner or a questionable situation.

When you are giving your undivided attention to making a decision yet never making it, you are likely to feel that your relationship with Spirit is on hold. This can be very aggravating, causing your daily life to feel upsetting and your mind to drive you crazy with deliberations. At the core of every challenging decision is the desire for something simple and the fear that you can't have it. When you can't make up your mind you are usually hoping for love, success, or contentment but tortured with the idea that a wrong choice will ruin your chances.

It is important to remember that love's source is love itself, so any choice made of love will bring love. Success comes from being willing to fail as well as being willing to succeed, so you will have success in time if you keep taking steps forward. Even the wrong step will bring you closer to success because it will teach you to take another step that is more success-oriented. Contentment will only come from peace of heart and mind. You will naturally be closer to contentment once you make a choice.

When you make a choice from love and stay committed to living that choice from love, you will experience deep security and love. Love is only disrupted when we choose to be in a mode of fear. The feeling of security is only disrupted when we choose to be uncommitted to the choice we have made.

Perhaps you are now thinking, "How can this be true? I was committed to my wife and she had an affair. I was committed to my profession and I got fired. I was committed to my church and they kicked me out when they discovered I was gay." You will have your own story of disappointment, as we all do.

You think you were committed to your wife, your career, and your church, but these people and places were actually components of a larger commitment. When you are committed to love, you will stay in a state of love under all circumstances. When you are committed to upset, you will stay in a state of upset under all circumstances.

The maple trees in Maryland, where I grew up, remained strong and secure throughout the seasons. They were abundant with nourishing green in the summer, celebratory with multiple colors in the autumn, lonely and available for receiving the comforting blanket of white snow in the winter, and sweetly offering little helicopter seed pods for everyone who sought refuge in their shade in the spring. During all of their fleeting moods of existence they remained sturdy and strong. You will remain at core what you are committed to while the scenes of your life play are in flux. If you live and feel your life play with love, you will know love. If you live and feel your life play from the heart of hunger and disappointment, you will know hunger and disappointment, regardless of the circumstances.

A person who has been betrayed can feel the sorrow of that betrayal, yet also feel gratitude for all the gifts he has received from a partner and life itself. There are always many gifts for which to be thankful, including all the gifts of personality we receive from others and all the gifts we are able to give others due to the grace of personality traits Spirit has given us. Another person's words of care are gemstones. Your kindness is gold. The miracle of life itself is an eternal holiday.

If you don't know what you are committed to, look at your life and it will tell you. My sister was born with multiple mental and physical disabilities, and she manages to have a very constructive and happy life. She has friends, a job, and many talents. She plays piano, travels, sings in a musical theater troupe, swims, and works on a computer. This is because she is committed to positivity. I have met people with fewer obstacles in their lives who are consistently bored, depressed, and unhappy because they are committed to misery. They are not bad people for being committed to misery. They simply lack the support and tools for being committed to success. When you are committed to happiness you will find many reasons to be happy. When you are committed to getting support, it will come. Change your life story, and the life play will begin to change itself. Focus on what is good in your life and you will get more of it.

When you are having trouble deciding about a partner, job, or something else, it is important to ask yourself, "What am I committed to?" The answer must be a theme rather than a subject. In other words, if you are committed to love, love is your theme and the people and places and events you love are the subjects. Ask yourself, "What do I most deeply want to experience, give, or receive in this decision? Is it love? Is it cooperation?"

Don't try to make rules about the particulars such as, "I want to experience cooperation with Tim at 2 PM regarding painting the club house. Furthermore, Tim must cooperate by using the brush stroke that I prefer." These kinds of demands, which we all make whether or not we consciously express them, are apt to bring disappointment. Instead, decide to experience cooperation as a way of life. If you commit to being cooperative, you will build more and more cooperative moments in your life, attract others who are cooperative, and lose interest when people are not.

Once you are clear about the basic intention desired in your life, it will be much easier to actualize it. Greta was in agony about which boyfriend to commit to. She had become involved with two men. She thought that the problem was choosing between a fun boyfriend and a better listener. When she realized that she was committed to happiness she realized that she could have happiness with either of these men. She chose the boyfriend who was a better listener and made a conscious choice to initiate more fun in that relationship. Greta made sure that both of her needs were met and she was happy.

Rob couldn't decide about proposing to his girlfriend, Laurel, or not proposing. When I asked what was he scared of, he said "being disappointed." When I asked him to clarify what he might become disappointed about, he said "not getting enough love." When I asked him to tell me what it was that he desired, he said "enough love."

Rob immediately realized that he was postponing making a commitment to a loving relationship from fear of not being loved and in the process he was contributing fear and lack of love to his life on his own. He decided to propose to his girlfriend, show his commitment to their love, and, of course, he got a lot more love in return. Laurel was a loving person, so his generosity inspired even more generosity in her. Give love and that is what you will receive. On the other hand, when you give love and someone repeatedly takes advantage of it, get out. A loving person can easily attract another loving person if he or she is willing to receive as well as to give, so release anyone who is not playing the same game of life as you.

If you are committed to love or gratitude or joy and you find yourself disappointed by someone, the experience will be a learning gift and you will continue to experience love, gratitude, and joy even if you go through temporary sadness. Once you make a choice, you will immediately be shown what motivates you to make the choice and what is motivating other people involved in the choice. Consequently, your choice will bring you rewards right away. If the choice is made from love, you will feel love. If the choice is made from anger, you will immediately feel anger. If you give your best and someone takes advantage of you, you will know that you must move on, but your love will never be destroyed. You simply give it to someone who is more deserving.

Jamie feared that he would be unhappy if he got married, so he dated numerous women, caused all kinds of melodramas, and suffered. Meanwhile, a good friend of his chose to marry a woman he loved and to give love and commitment to the relationship. In doing so, he felt love and security. He had his ups and downs and did not have a perfect relationship, but overall he experienced peace. Jamie, the man who let his fear of loss drive his decisions, received from life exactly what he most feared: repeated abandonment and betrayal. Lost in his own sabotage, he felt let down again and again.

In a time when choices are abundant, choosing a career, choosing a mate, and even choosing a place to live can be a tormenting process. When you are struggling with a decision it is important to go back to your basic intention. What is your primary desire?

One way to avoid problems is to take each of the personality types' questions into account first. Sharon had a habit of making quick decisions with a lot of enthusiasm and questioning them later. Leaving questions out of her initial process caused her pain that could have been avoided. At one point in her life she agreed to start a clinic with a friend of hers. After the first year of arduous work that starting a business entails, she realized that she was yearning to live a simple life. If her business succeeded, she would spend the next twenty years in the middle of Silicon Valley, a place for which she had no exuberance. She was faced with a decision of leaving her business partner with an extreme amount of work or moving forward toward a life that would not be pleasurable to her.

The next time that she was about to jump on a new plan, she decided to incorporate the Creative Decision-Making process first. This process has two parts. The first part involved requires looking at the decision as though you are standing in the chakra of each of the Creative Personality Types. Before deciding yes or no, ask yourself all of the following questions. These questions are compiled from the focuses of each of the Creative Personality Types. After answering the questions consult with your inner baby, child, teenager, and adult prior to implementing final decisions.

Creative Decision-Making Step One
Questions to Answer Before Making a Decision
Actor Will this decision lead to a life in which I will be able to adequately express myself? In what ways will this decision contribute to or challenge this? Are the challenges worth taking on, or are they unnecessary obstacles to my values?

Dancer What feelings might I experience if I make this decision? Will I feel good about this decision?

Critic Once the decision is made, what improvements will be necessary? Are there matters I need to address before making this decision?

Score Composer What is my ideal dream in relationship to this decision, and will this decision help me create that dream or take me away from it?

Set Designer What are the practical matters involved in this decision? What will need to be done to make it happen? Am I willing to do what it truly takes?

Stage Manager What kind of help will I need to carry out this decision? How will I find this help? Am I willing to receive and give the needed help?

Playwright What is the story I am telling myself about this decision? Knowing myself, is my story likely to change as realities come to fruition?

Director How will this decision affect others? Is this a decision that will be in the best interest of everyone involved?

Lighting Designer What is the most positive viewpoint I have about this decision? What is the most negative one? What is the middle ground? In the face of obstacles, will I be ready to stay positively focused on living with this decision?

Sound Designer When I meditate on this decision, what mood do I experience?

Promoter When I tell others about this decision, what do I have to say about it that is inspiring? Is anything I am likely to say destined to convince others that not doing it would be more enlivening than doing it?

Audience Member Can I respect and encourage myself about this decision regardless of the outcome?

■ ■ ■

By answering the above questions, you will take into account your different desires, expectations, and possible pitfalls, thus determining if you are fully available to live with the consequences.

Creative Decision-Making Step Two
Address Different Parts of Yourself Before Making a Final Decision: Consult the Inner Baby, Child, Teenager, and Adult

A decision that leads to disappointment is often the result of adhering to one part of yourself while ignoring the others. The adult in you may decide that you need to do a two-year graduate program in one year so that you will finish earlier. Halfway into the year of unyielding mental work, your child self may be exasperated from no play and get sick. By consulting your inner baby, child, teenager, and adult, and getting their insights before making a final decision, you are likely to choose a route with which you can be at peace in the long run.

Find a quiet place where you can meditate, write, or engage in an artistic endeavor. Allow yourself to express each inner part of you through imagination, writing, or your preferred type of art. You will learn more about your own needs by creatively expressing parts of yourself from previous stages in your life.

Steps for Creative Decision-Making

- Utilize wisdom from each of the Creative Personality Types.
- Consult with your inner baby, child, teenager, and adult.

■ ■ ■

Geoff, an intern, made a decision to co-lead a therapy group because his adult self knew that it would be a good experience. Deep inside, however, he had uncomfortable feelings that he did not address. He made the commitment without communicating his concern to anyone else. Halfway through the therapy meetings, he disappeared from the group. His co-leader felt betrayed and his clients felt confused and abandoned. He dismantled his own credibility. The co-leader and the director of the counseling agency knew they could not rely upon him. Had he paid attention to the feeling in his gut and processed it with the co-leader, he could have helped the inner child to get what he needed. Instead, his confusion caused upset for others.

When we take the time to look at our doubts, we can either address them in a way that alleviates them or we can make a decision not to enter territory that will stir them up, consequently making a more durable decision.

Of course, no decision is perfect and most require adjustment once made. All decisions offer unexpected elements as well. However, preparing for the decision by looking at factors in advance gets you in the mode of responding positively to challenging and unforeseen events, as well as allows you to make a decision more realistically.

If a decision is made with unexamined motives you may not be fulfilled in the long run. This is because your decision gives back to you exactly what you give to it. Decisions are like children. Loved children are loving. Children who are given structure and guidelines are secure. Use your love and your practicality to make a decision. Be as honest with yourself as possible. If fear is motivating your decision in any of its numerous forms (see chart in Chapter Three), you are better off addressing your fears now.

If you aren't sure about how you made a decision, look at what is reflected back at you. Your eyes allow you to look fully at everyone but yourself, so use the world around you as a mirror. Whatever you see is you. If you see something you don't like, you know you have the opportunity to help create a change or choose a different environment.

With Self-Awareness, Some People Stay Successful When Their Motive and the Outcome Don't Match. Here's How:

- Identify your supposed motive.
- Look honestly at how you are off track.
- Recommit to your motive (your essential purpose), regardless of the fleeting external circumstances.

When deliberating between one choice or another, it is important to get to the basics. Most choices revolve around seven different core categories. By breaking a decision into the seven core categories, whether it is a decision about choosing a mate, a job, or a school for your child, you will gain perspective. You will see that external factors are either favorable or unfavorable and that choosing the most favorable is what you want. Internal factors will cloud your thinking if they are not clearly addressed. By directly addressing yourself, you can change what you bring to a situation, and feel more competent about your decision, as a result.

First look at the area of grace and mystery. Is something pulling you towards that decision that goes beyond your intellect? If so, the decision will bring you an opportunity for growth. If not, the decision may lead to a feeling of boredom.

Second, look at the area of wisdom. If you decide to marry your boyfriend, will you feel satisfied in the area of wisdom? Do both of you bring wisdom to each other that is supportive? If so, you are setting up a desirable life. If not, you are forgetting to plan ahead in your best interest.

Next look at the area of communication. If your child goes to the private school, will her teacher speak to her in a manner that is positive? If so, you are making a decision that will give her a favorable experience. If not, you are making a decision that will cause her trouble.

How about love? Is the love between you and the person you are going to live with strong? If so, you are giving yourself the gift of feeling good in your heart. If not, you are putting yourself in a situation that will be lacking.

What about power and emotions? Does the mutual chemistry between you and the others in the start-up company contribute to well-being and productivity? If yes, you are making a choice that will naturally lead to feelings of vitality. If not, you are choosing to take on a job that will zap you of your energy.

How about passion? Do you feel enlivened when you think about the major you are considering for college? If yes, you are choosing a good major for yourself. If no, you are setting yourself up for a tedious couple of years in school not to mention your future career.

What about lifestyle compatibility? Do you and the person you wish to date have similar lifestyle interests? If you do, you will be happy with how you share your time. If you don't, you will be disappointed and end up alone much of the time.

Seven Significant Aspects to Review in Any Decision

1 Grace and mystery
2 Wisdom
3 Communication
4 Love
5 Power
6 Passion
7 Practicality

Incompatible Partners and Situations

An inability to solve a conflict can be the unchangeable result of two people with fundamentally different lifestyle choices who would be better off apart. A colleague with different values than the others in the office is in a similar situation and needs to consider switching jobs. When changing yourself and your actions would violate your soul-calling or a moral belief you hold, and not changing your role and actions leaves the problem unsolved, you need to come to terms with having chosen an incompatible life partner (or group of people, in the case of a career).

In this case your options are 1) choose to live with the disappointment, accepting it as a feeling you will have throughout life but commit yourself to not making it worse with obsessive complaining; 2) ask your partner to make a compromise for your sake and find out if she or he can without violating one of her or his own basic values; or 3) accept that you are incompatible and that you made a mistake, but that it has led you to know more about your relationship needs so that you are prepared to make a better decision in the future.

Making the Decision About Leaving or Staying

You have one of three choices. Avoiding them will only postpone the process.

- Choose to live with the disappointment.
- Co-create a compromise.
- Forgive yourself for choosing someone with whom you are not compatible and lovingly move on.

■ ■ ■

Are you a stranger or a friend to Spirit? Are you a stranger or a friend to yourself? How about to others? Your life is full of paragraphs and paragraphs of living. You may write these in a happy way. Someday, if not already, your hands will be full of lines that tell of your life journeys. Do the paragraphs and lines take you closer or further to the sound of Spirit beating a joyous drum of music in your heart? You decide each moment.

9 · Creative Projects

Alternatives to Ongoing Conflict
With the Help of Artistic Media

You have now learned that altering a problem requires altering your role in it. When you believe that you are a Director in your life play rather than a cast character, you will alter your role and thereby alter the story of your life. Artistic projects can help you do this.

Whenever you believe that someone else or something else is responsible for your well-being, you lose the ability to treat your life as a creative opportunity. Utilizing a creative mode gives your mind a break from internal reruns of your personal soap opera.

Turning away from the world of intellect and explanations and into the world of creativity and the subconscious can offer unexpected solutions and experiences. You and your partner will find an easier merging point when you say goodbye to the same old thoughts about your problems. By relaxing into a new mode of creativity, you can discuss solutions with new inspiration and motivation. You can do this with artistic projects such as visual art, dance, drama, music, or writing.

When addressing your problems with art, you give your mind a rest. You are likely to find yourself breaking old patterns and feeling enlivened with new possibilities. By involving yourself in a creative project you are apt to discover new emotional responses to old situations.

The first part of this chapter gives you creative projects to do that expand your wisdom in each of the Creative Personality Types' area. These exercises include acting, drawing, dancing, writing, critiquing, expressing, helping, vocalizing, perceiving, meditating, and listening. Choose the exercises that appeal to you.

The second part of this chapter teaches you how to use art, drama, dance, and music to alter your feelings, get closer to your partner, and heal emotional aches and pains that have been left unrepaired from the past. It is not necessary to have artistic training, skill, or talent to use these mediums in a therapeutic way. It is also not necessary to engage in the projects in the second part of this chapter to derive significant help from this book. Try them if you are drawn to any of them and would like to experiment with your growth process in a new way.

Fun and Artistic Exercises To Alter a Conflict Using the Creative Personality Types' Methods

Actor Create a character that would respond to your situation in a very different manner than you. Act out your new character's response. When you allow yourself to try out a new response to an old situation, the situation will change.

Dancer Improvise a dance that fully expresses the feelings you are experiencing in response to the situation you are encountering in your life. When a feeling is fully expressed, it naturally changes. Dance until the feelings begin to change.

Critic Write a review about your own behavior in the play of satisfaction. What are you doing or not doing to add or subtract from your own happiness? When you critique your own participation instead of the world around you, you are apt to lead yourself to a happier mode of involvement in your own life.

Score Composer Experiment with your own voice tones, aiming to express your ideal world through sound. Go into your heart to search for a quality that will make life ideal. Put the warmth of that quality into your voice when you speak. When we offer tones that speak to people's hearts and joy, a situation can easily change for the best.

Promoter Make a poster that includes a list of special things your partner has done for you that have given you happiness. Post it where your partner can see it. Letting someone know that they are appreciated leads to more love and gratitude.

Set Designer Build or redesign something that will contribute to you and your partner's well-being. When you contribute to your shared environment with action, your sense of contentment will naturally increase.

Stage Manager Help your partner with something that is important to her or temporarily abandon your own troubles and help someone else who can use a hand. By putting focus on someone else for a while, you will get a new perspective on your own situation.

Playwright Rewrite the story of your life so that it is the way you desire. Your recorded thoughts can naturally lead toward new actions and new situations.

Director Take a new look at the old situation. Instead of viewing the problem as your personal problem, look at it as a shared problem. Create a new solution that involves consideration of both of you. Write the solution down.

Lighting Designer Take a new look at the situation. Focus on everything that you can be grateful about and draw a picture to express this gratitude. When you focus on what you appreciate more of it comes your way.

Sound Designer Create the feeling you would like to have by taping different sounds and pieces of music. You can listen to sounds that lead you to carry a warm feeling inside. Your internal mood will silently and naturally rub off on others.

Audience Member Listen to your partner with different ears by pretending that you are a TV interviewer and she is your interviewee. Your job is to receive her with acceptance and respect. Video the interview taking both roles (the interviewer and interviewee).

Using Art Media for Individual Emotional Catharsis

It is very valuable to express your individual feelings with an art project before approaching your partner in the face of a conflict. By doing this, you take responsibility for your own feelings rather than inflicting them entirely on your partner. Your emotions always belong to you and are yours to resolve. When you neglect to release your emotions you are more likely to get into arguments that escalate.

Once you have given yourself a way to get your emotions out, it will be a lot easier to talk to your partner in a constructive and positive manner. Your partner, who will feel respected rather than attacked, will be more likely to respond to you with respect as opposed to defensiveness.

One couple, Nancy and Eric, used painting and dance to address their feelings before coming to conclusions about the relationship. Had they let their disappointment and anger inform their communication and decisions, their relationship may have ended prematurely. Instead, both decided to use an art medium as a means of catharsis. By doing so, each arrived at a positive place, and both were able to clear their misunderstandings with each other.

Eric and Nancy delighted in an immediately passionate and comfortable connection with each other when they met at a party in Felton, California, Nancy's hometown. Eric was visiting friends but lived three hours away. Nancy's ease with herself was delightful to him. "Your passion is so accessible to you," he said. The feelings that Nancy had for Eric were deliciously new to her. Never had she felt so in love and deeply free to express herself to someone so quickly.

She decided to surprise Eric with a visit a week later. He lived three hours away, so it would be a trek. She spent her week fantasizing about appearing on his doorstep. She dreamed about the joy that his face would radiate when she arrived.

The next weekend she woke up early, drove all the way to Calistoga, and knocked on his door.

"Who is it?" came a muffled voice through the door.

"It's Nancy."

"I'm busy," he said.

Heartbroken and shocked, Nancy turned around and drove back home. Her first thought was to forget about the jerk forever. For the next week, she put all of his messages on save without listening to them and did not call him. She was furious.

The next weekend at the exact time of her disillusionment the previous weekend, she decided to paint her feelings. By painting her anger, she allowed herself to fully experience it, and it began to subside. As she painted, her anger turned to sadness. By painting the sadness, she began to feel relieved.

Your feelings are like little children who simply want to express themselves and move along in the flow of life. When a small child cries, laughs, or rages, she releases emotional tension and goes back to a state of love. In our culture we are expected to contain our emotions without any kind of ceremonial outlets. This is like expecting a tree to stay healthy without letting it drop its leaves to make room for new buds. It leads to frustration and dissatisfaction. Emotion expressed leads to a light-hearted existence.

With a mode of expression for her emotion, Nancy's thoughts switched from how awful Eric was to curiosity about what his side of the story was. Was he involved with someone in Calistoga? Was she invasive for showing up without an invitation?

Her heart began to remember that her initial feeling about Eric was good and warm. Her intuition had told her that he was a very caring person. During the short time that she spent with him he presented himself to be solid and thoughtful. Something just wasn't making sense.

She continued to spontaneously paint. To her surprise, the painting switched from sadness to an expression of the shared strength and joy she had felt with Eric at the party. In painting, she recalled her first connection with Eric deeply. She decided to listen to his messages.

Eric's messages were all from the East Coast. Eric had to suddenly fly to Massachusetts, where his best friend had been critically injured in an accident. Eric had asked a neighbor's teenage son to house-sit and take care of his pets. The person who had been too busy to answer the door was not Eric, but the house-sitter. Nancy's trust in her intuition and use of creative language led her back to a place of love, which revealed the truth of the situation.

While Nancy was on an emotional journey, Eric had left ten messages for her. The first five were full of love and compliments. Eric was overwhelmed with the love he felt toward this new woman in his life. He assumed that she felt the same way. After calling her for five days in a row and not hearing back once, he became despondent. I must be full of myself, he thought. My imagination is crazy. Obviously it was a one-sided love affair.

After reaching a point of excruciating pain, Eric decided to put on a headset, go into his best friend's basement, and dance. He danced for two hours straight. He cried. He punched a punching bag. When he was finished dancing, he felt renewed. He didn't want to give up. He called Nancy again and this time she answered the phone. Having released their emotions, both Nancy and Eric were receptive and kind toward each other. Nancy and Eric chose to paint and dance, but any art form would have worked. They saved their relationship by individually addressing their emotions and coming to each other from a place of personal peace and care.

Co-Creating with Art Media to Improve Understanding and Intimacy

Co-Creating with Visual Art

It is common and easy to turn an argument into a very serious part of life. It is more fun, and often more productive, to do something positive and creative as a method of addressing a problem. One couple shared in the creation of a visual art project as a means of turning a chronic problem around. This couple had outstanding results.

Ellen and Brian turned a disheartening struggle into deeper understanding and mutual support by learning to look at their situation through Directors' eyes and then playing with art. Ellen and Brian had been married for three years but were on the verge of a divorce. A relationship that started out with mutual admiration and shared life-goals had become a series of disappointments. Three years of unsatisfied needs were pulling them apart. Their problems had become their emotional food, and the sustenance of their relationship was conflict.

Many of us start a relationship with a delicious dream and end up with a compost pile. Compost in itself is a natural part of life and the source of healthy soil. During the first counseling session, Ellen explained her view of her problem with her beloved. "When Brian and I met, we spoke for hours about our dreams and wishes for a life mate. We seemed to share the same desires. For example, both of us value city life. We want to raise a family in the city, where our children can be exposed to culture, politics, and art. We both love to camp, ski, and snorkel. He's the first boyfriend who shares my love of both summer and winter sports. Both of us paint as a hobby. We're both Jewish and want to raise Jewish children."

Brian agreed with Ellen's perceptions and added some more. "Ellen and I have similar values regarding community, also. I'm a director and producer for public access television. She's a photographer with a focus on local community. We both value careers based on serving our community. Both of us want to have two children. Both of us believe in a committed monogamous marriage, yet value platonic friendships with the opposite sex."

From here, this couple's conversation escalated into an angry argument because neither was listening with the intent to respond to the other's needs. Both Ellen and Brian were focused on defending themselves. Two Lighting Designers were set on maintaining their own perspectives and consequently butting heads.

"But in day-to-day life we don't get along," Ellen said. "When Brian gets home he turns on the television. I want to be close."

Brian responded, "I'm tired after working a ten-hour day. I want some time to myself. I've been juggling people all day long. I want to see how some of the shows I worked on came out. Ellen doesn't seem interested in my work. I want to come home to someone who cares about what I have been doing all day."

"Brian, you know that's because I want us to make time for each other. I want to know how your day was by talking to you. How can I when you are staring at a television set?"

"That's what weekends are for," Brian said. "Weekends are family time. When we got married we said we would have a regular Shabbat, and we never do. During the work week I am exhausted. I need to unwind. I just need to space out with the TV for a while. I'm tired. If you would stop hounding me and give me time to restore myself, I would be well and ready to give you lots of attention on the weekend. Why do you always bring a zoo of people over when the weekend comes if you want to have time for ourselves?"

"My family isn't a zoo of people. You knew I had a close extended family when you got together with me. Shabbat is family time. Besides, my family has helped us out quite a bit. Who paid for our honeymoon and wedding? Who split the down payment on our home? What do you think it's like to be married to a man whose family could care less about us? When we have children, I won't be able to call your parents or brother and sisters to help out. My family will be a steady part of their upbringing."

"Your family doesn't give me room to breathe. When we have children, I will be their father. Your family won't."

Months of bickering were getting this couple deeper and deeper into a marriage of dissatisfaction, and they both knew it. Complaints only led to more complaints. Insults only led to mutual dissatisfaction. When Ellen brought up the possibility of divorce, they looked into each other's green eyes and knew that something more important than disappointment was keeping them together, even though lately, it seemed that marriage was nothing more. Their relationship had started with dreams and mutual adoration. For a couple with so much in common, they were astounded at how much they now argued. Both of them wanted to return to loving each other and building dreams together.

Ellen and Brian came up with a unique way to address their conflict using art. By understanding the basis of their process, you may be able to address conflicts with your partner in a positive way, regardless of whether or not you want to utilize art yourselves. In spite of disappointments, this couple made a painting that represented the positive feelings they had toward their relationship. One third of the painting was Ellen's, one third was Brian's, and the middle was combined. When the painting was complete, they put it up across from the bed so it would become the first thing each saw when waking up in the morning. Then they got into their bed, cuddled up together facing the painting, and took turns offering appreciation for each other's contributions to the relationship. Looking at images of two lovers hugging (Eric's image) and a woman reaching her arms into the air with flowers (Ellen's expression of thanks) inspired joy in each of them.

Good moods developed from expressing appreciation. Feeling appreciated, both of them were more responsive to each other's requests. Ellen thanked Brian for giving her space when she did want privacy. When she focused on the positive instead of the negative, she realized that his family's absence had encouraged her to become a more independent adult, which felt empowering. Being the youngest in a close family, she frequently adopted the advice of her parents and siblings instead of using her own judgment. Observing the ways that Brian thought out everything for himself had caused her to do more of the same. She felt a sense of pride when she chose interior decorations for her studio instead of taking the hand-me-downs her Mom brought her. She felt liberated by taking time to think out some business decisions rather than immediately getting on the phone with all of her older siblings.

Brian thanked Ellen for being so easy to be close to, making herself consistently emotionally available, and for her family's deep love and care. He said he was learning to be closer and more loving because of her and her family, and if he was overwhelmed and unable to match her at times he was sorry. Her openness was very new to him.

Ellen offered to reserve Saturdays for them to have alone. Brian offered to spend some time with her when he came home in the evenings, rather than going straight to the television set.

Ellen asked Brian to reach out to her family more. He said that he was willing to. Brian asked Ellen to take more interest in his career. She said she would.

They decided to continue this process regularly. Every Saturday morning they shared appreciation, offerings, and requests with each other. Their relationship became rewarding to them. They came to see that their main problem had not been different desires but rather focusing on what wasn't working without focusing on how to change it. At the core, each wanted to be happy and experience a better situation. This combined with fear instead of love led them to disappointment and the verge of despair. Substituting love into the equation in place of fear changed the outcome one hundred percent.

Steps for Co-Creating an Art Project to Improve Intimacy

- Divide your canvas into three sections with a charcoal-drawn line.
- Each person can paint feelings of gratitude about the other on a different portion of the canvas.

- Together, paint your feelings of gratitude toward the relationship in the third portion of the canvas.
- After finishing the painting, find a cozy place to cuddle up and look at it together. As you look, take turns giving verbal appreciation, offerings of compromises that will serve your partner, and requests of your partner. Make sure to respond to each others' appreciation, offerings, and requests.
- Set aside a weekly appointment or other regularly scheduled time to repeat step four of this exercise. If you get stuck in your old habits, you can repeat the creation process, this time focusing on a particular aspect of your relationship.

The above exercise can also be practiced with drama, dance, writing, or music by taking the following steps.

Co-Creating with Drama
- Have each partner go into a separate room and develop a character who easily expresses appreciation of his or her partner.
- Have your characters meet, perform, and listen to each other's monologues.
- Have your characters interactively converse about their appreciation.
- Find a cozy place to cuddle up together. Take turns giving verbal appreciation, as yourself, offerings of compromises that will serve your partner, and requests of your partner. Make sure to respond to each other's appreciation, offerings, and requests.

- Set aside a weekly appointment or other regularly scheduled time to repeat step four of this exercise. If you get stuck in your old habits, you can repeat the creation process, this time focusing on a particular aspect of your relationship.

Co-Creating with Dance

- Have each partner go into a separate room and choreograph a dance that expresses appreciation toward the other.
- Reconvene and perform the dances for each other.
- Improvise a dance together using moves from both of your dance pieces.
- See the last two items on the bulleted list for "Co-Creating with Drama".

Co-Creating with Music

- Have each partner go into a separate room and make up a song or piece of music that expresses appreciation for his or her partner.
- Come back together and share the music with each other, one at a time.
- Find ways to combine parts of each other's music to create a song or music piece together.
- See the last two items on the bulleted list for "Co-Creating with Drama".

Co-Creating with Writing

- Each person write a poem, story, essay, or list of appreciation to express gratitude to his or her partner.
- Share what you have written.

- Write a piece together using what each of you has already written to express gratitude about the relationship.
- See the last two items on the bulleted list for "Co-Creating with Drama".

Dance and Music Project

Candy and Grant were so fed up with each other that they came to counseling as a last resort. The unhappiness they shared had sunk so low that neither could clearly articulate what the problem was from a solution-oriented perspective. They had become so focused on their disappointment with marriage that they fed it, lived in it, and watched it increase.

Grant was certain that the problem was Candy, who "didn't appreciate him for who he was."

Candy was sure that Grant was causing their conflict by "being grumpy."

Grant wasn't a trained drummer, but he loved to play around with his daughter's collection of percussion instruments to ease his mind.

Candy loved to take dance classes and dance in clubs. This couple used music and dance to alter their problem.

Grant and Candy imitated how their conversations often went by using the percussion instruments and Candy's dancing. They replicated a conversation as they experienced it without using words and videotaped it.

Candy danced the way she felt in conversations with Grant. Grant drummed the way he felt in conversations with Candy. Upon seeing themselves on video, both of them became more interested in what she or he was doing and less focused on what the other was doing. Candy realized that every time Grant tried to initiate contact she distanced herself by fleeing into her own world. Grant noticed that every time Candy tried to uplift his spirits he tried to pull her into his depression.

They decided to be playful with the dance/percussion conversation. Candy found that by joining with Grant in his rhythm she could lead him into a fun, more light-hearted dance. Grant found that surrendering to Candy's cheerful movement gave him a lot more pleasure than trying to pull her into his weighted-down existence.

The couple then discussed ways that they could bring this type of interaction into day-to-day life. Grant said that he would go with Candy's whimsical invitations into silly conversations and fun activities. Once he did this, he found that his wife was capable of leading him to great joy. Joy is actually what he truly desired when he pulled her into his depression. He just hadn't realized it. Pulling someone along when you are sinking is a common, yet unconscious, cry for assistance. Assistance is everywhere once you are able to take it.

Candy chose to make eye contact with her husband and listen to him caringly. Distancing herself and spinning into her own playful world whenever he was depressed was an attempt to keep herself free of his depression. It backfired, however, because he felt rejected and became more invested in pulling her in. When she took a moment to make genuine contact, he was able to come along for her happier ride.

Writing and Drama Project

Joan and Donald had been in limbo for eight years. They met in their mid-twenties. At thirty-three and thirty-four, neither was ready to get married or to break up, although neither was satisfied with their current unsettled relationship.

Donald had been a professional actor from age twenty-two to thirty-one. Their problems began when he became a mortgage broker and was not happy with his life. He worked very hard and was unusually successful, but he wasn't fulfilled.

Joan loved to write in her journal so she decided to write down daily fantasies of how her perfect life with Donald could be. She threw away a previous journal filled with complaints. Joan invited Donald to hear the fantasies and act them out with her. He loved the idea. Acting gave him joy and released the tension at the end of his day with finances.

This couple's recovery was easy. They had been happy and poor for years and quickly turned unhappy on the way to being well off. In using the journal writing and acting, this couple quickly realized that their problems were the result of Donald's unhappiness. Joan, who had a one-woman landscaping business, was barely making minimum wage after business expenses, but she was fulfilled with life. Joan realized she resented Donald for not being so himself. She wanted her old boyfriend back. Donald, aware of the money it would require to have a family, had taken on new responsibility at the sacrifice of his joy and resented Joan for neither encouraging nor appreciating this.

By focusing on what Joan wanted, Donald became more able to clearly articulate what he wanted. The couple decided to share responsibilities more equally. Donald worked half time, thus becoming able to resume acting. Joan set her mind to making her business more effective and committed to spending more hours each week promoting herself by writing articles, attending mixers, and writing press releases. The couple was married within six months.

Still Stuck?

An inability to solve a partner relational problem can be the result of an unresolved individual problem. If you have determined that you need to do some work on an unresolved childhood problem, the following art project will be of use. This project is designed for you to do alone. It will help you work through your personal unmet needs.

The first part of the exercise is letting go of what is causing you pain. Before you can listen to a new solution, you must eject the old problem. You must let go of what you don't want. This is done through expression. Choose an art medium and use it to express what you wish to release. Do you want to release fear, despair, anger, sorrow, impatience, jealousy, or something else? If it is something else, what is it?

Choose a time slot three to five days a week during which you can take ten minutes to express what is disturbing you. Be patient with yourself and allow the release to take as much time as it needs. You can't choose how many days, months, years, or decades you will need to give this expression the time it deserves. You can count on feeling a lot more nourished, inspired, and alive, however, when you do choose to give yourself the gift of expressing.

Don't think of letting go as pushing away. Ironically, letting go comes from embracing. Think of what you want to release as a beautiful baby who needs your care. You can think of it as a cat, dog, garden, precious possession, or whatever calls forth your care. Accept and love that expression as something cherished. This is different than feeding it. You make it grow bigger by adding complaints to it. You give it what it's longing for by loving it. When you love what you thought you hated, it becomes your friend. You discover that your rejection of yourself was actually the source of your discomfort and not the part of yourself that you thought you disliked.

If you think of this exercise as a race to an end, you will get frustrated. Think of it as a transformative process, a part of your life journey that is a treasure to experience, with surprises and gifts on the way. Though contrary to the quick pace and fast results desired in Western culture, continuing this process consistently for months or even years will increase results and effectiveness in all areas of life.

Now sit quietly, focus on your heart, and thank life for the opportunity to learn to grow with the wisdom you are receiving from this part of you.

Then using the art form of your choice, spend ten to thirty minutes expressing the part of you that you had previously wanted to diminish.

Paint the color and shapes you see in it. Move the motion you feel in it. Play the sound you hear in it. Become the character that embodies it. Write the poetry that speaks it. This is a sacred time, a private time, so ask Spirit to be present with you.

A feeling that is exuberantly or excruciatingly deep comes from long ago, perhaps from childhood, perhaps from ancestral blood, perhaps from another existence, or perhaps from others if you are especially sensitive and empathetic. The more you allow it to exist with your love, the more you will be able to give and take in love, and the core of your partner's care for you will become apparent.

The second part of this exercise is to spend half of your private expression time creating what you do want. Finding more happiness with another requires knowing what you want. Do you want love, nourishment, sex, and care? When we release we must also create so that we don't fill ourselves back up with the same thing. Spend half of your session expressing what you want to know and feel.

If you don't know what you want, it's probably the opposite of what you don't want. So if you don't want distrust you probably want trust. Use the chart in Chapter 3 to help you.

How To Move Beyond Being Stuck
- Identify the part of you that is troubling you.
- Give that part of you full expression through a creative project. (Plan ten to thirty minutes that you will work on the project daily for at least one week.)
- Spend equal time each day creatively expressing what it is that you want. Make sure that you identify what you do and

don't want in the simplest terms. When you say you want money, you probably want security or happiness or freedom. When you say you don't want to have an argument, you probably don't want to experience anger. Simplify.

- If you do this process and it becomes uncomfortable or overwhelming, arrange to see a psychotherapist, a coach, or a counselor.

■ ■ ■

Communication isn't just a formula. Use the formulas to improve communication, but just as importantly, bring yourself to the picture. Your life with another is like a performance art piece that you can develop in your own unique way. When you look at your relationship as an opportunity to play and turn dreams into life, conflicts are simply opportunities for something better than you ever experienced before. Make the most of your relationship, and life will make the most of you. Bless your relationship with the best of yourself, and the rewards will be profound. Choose a mate who is doing the same, and heaven will be your home here on Earth.

When the air becomes stale with disappointments of years, cleanse yourself with true tears. When you realize that you have clenched yourself into your conversation like a fist unable to love, sob deeply. Then you will soften; your breath will become like a child's. Now you can offer acts of love. Reach out your hands; paint the set yellow, and the goodness of each other will rise in your body like the sun.

10 · Creative Intimacy

Making the Most of Relationship Opportunities

If you want to be happy in relationship, realize that relationship is an arena in which you learn another's language. Jerry felt that promises and commitments were the most important part of a relationship. Tabatha felt that joy and fun were essential. For a while they became skeptical of their compatibility. Jerry said that Tabatha wasn't grown up, and Tabatha said that Jerry was an old fuddy-duddy. These judgments contributed nothing but bad feelings to the relationship. Both participants decided to celebrate each other instead of judge each other. The judgments weren't getting them what they wanted. Jerry and Tabatha decided to have a commitment (pre-wedding) ritual in which they would speak their vows to each other. Jerry wrote the vows while Tabatha came up with ways to include friends and make it a fun day.

Jerry found that the spoken commitments felt deeper and more authentic when they were combined with all the sensory additions Tabatha brought. She had flowers for everyone, singers, poetry readers, and dancing. Tabatha found that the pleasure she received was deeper and fuller with the combined commitments and vows. For a while this couple used their differences to create unhappiness, but they realized there was no point to this. Jerry, the Playwright, and Tabatha, the Set Designer/Actor, made each other's world more delightful by receiving what each other had to give.

Be playful. Grace and Bradley kept fighting about sex.

"You always want it your way," Grace said.

"Actually, you're the boss in our relationship and our sex life. Everything that happens hinges on you," Bradley said.

"That's an unpleasant way to talk to me," Grace continued.

"Look who's talking," Bradley said.

This conversation, at very loud decibels, had become a regular weekend ritual. One day, Bradley came home and fed a chocolate-covered cherry to Grace.

"What would you like?" he asked. She showed him. She felt giddy and playful, and led him out to their private backyard. She pulled him toward her and rolled him around in the soft grass under the stars of a warm East Coast night. This was just the beginning of a wonderful decade and it was very simple.

Now their conversation goes like this: "Bradley, you always make lovemaking delightful!"

"Grace, you always make me feel wonderful."

Grace, the Critic/Dancer, and Bradley, the Director/Stage Manager, now devote their energy to making their relationship feel wonderful. They used to devote their energy to putting each other down, which never led to needs being met. If you are in a habit of complaining or putting your partner down, try using that same drive to praise, inquire, and raise your partner up. Watch the amazing difference. The strength of partnership comes in lifting each other up. Find the communication bridge. Is it more important to be the winner of a purposeless ongoing fight or to find a completely new approach that works? David was sure that Steve was being absurd. David and Steve had been vegetarians for eight years, and Steve served turkey every Thanksgiving to make David's parents feel at home. Every year they had a fight about this. "You're a hypocrite."

"Hypocrite? I'm the only one around here who thinks about others."

"Well I feel very neglected when you think about my parents more than me."

"More than you? I think about you 364 days a year, and the one day a year that your parents visit and you neglect them, I'm their personal waiter, host, and substitute son. I tell them about how wonderful you are, let them know about all the great things to do in town, and please them with food cooked with my favorite cookbooks."

After seven years of this unpleasant ordeal David said, "Can we talk more lovingly to each other this Thanksgiving?"

Steve said, "Yes."

David said, "It's not the turkey."

Steve said, "What is it?"

David, choosing to be brave, vulnerable, and wise, said, "My parents always wanted me to be the straight regular boy like my little brother and I couldn't do it. It's just not who I was. Now you behave just like my good little brother and they favor you."

"I'm sorry," said Steve, no longer angry with David for his turkey outbursts. "How can I support you and also be good to your parents?"

"You know what it really is?" David said. "It's that I've been mean to my parents in the same way they've been mean to me. I try to fit them into my mold and criticize them for not fitting. Although they initiated the negative communication, my pain has deepened over the years from doing it back to them. I'm going to cook the turkey with you this year. I'll switch the scenario around."

That was just the beginning of many unexpected Thanksgivings during which family ties got closer and deeper. David, the Playwright, and Steve, the Promoter/Set Designer, turned frustration into a satisfying solution. Always be the first to point communication back to a positive direction. You are full of love and fear, as is everyone else, so choose love at all times. Basically, life is a moment-to-moment choice between love and fear. Choose love because it feels ecstatic.

Attend to yourself. Julie cried for years because none of her boyfriends gave her the affection she desired. She broke up with all of them. Finally she decided to give herself the affection she desired. She paid for massages. She did lots of yoga. She cuddled with a new kitten. She hugged her friends regularly. She massaged and hugged her own body every night. Julie turned to the Dancer part of her personality in order to respond to her own needs. She drew upon the Lighting Designer part of her personality to focus on all the options that were available to her. She included the Sound Designer's wisdom in her healing process by turning to herself. The next boyfriend she met loved her body in a very warm, nourishing, and generous way. People respond to the messages we are giving out.

Know your purpose. Forget about the details of life. Carolina was upset because five of the twenty apple pies she made for her sister Diana's wedding got burned. Elana, Diana's other sister, who helped make the pies, was happy about how well fifteen of them came out. Carolina had an awful day. Elana had a spectacular day. When asked why she had a horrid day, Carolina said, "I ruined my sister's wedding." To her, the purpose of that day had become the perfection of the pies.

Elana said, "I contributed to the happiest day of my sister's life." To Elana, the purpose of that day had been adding to an already joyful day. The two sisters were at the same wedding, but each experienced a different play. Each was the Director of her own play on the very same stage. Each was a Playwright, but one chose a story of joy while the other chose a story of despair. Each experienced the results of what she chose as a central theme. Shed your light on your purpose with positivity and gratitude and you will feel deep delight.

Ask for support. Greta was despondent because nobody cared about her birthday. Roylie was elated because her birthday always lasted for weeks with gifts and dinners. Greta, tired of her miserable birthdays, called Roylie, wondering why their mutual friends cared so much more about her. "I think our friends love me, but on my birthday I wonder," Greta said.

Roylie explained that she began giving reminders that her birthday was coming two months in advance and continued until the night before. In her experience, people had enough to remember without being required to remember everyone's birthday, so she told everyone and they, of course, wanted to celebrate. Greta decided to host a party for herself. Almost everyone invited came, and for weeks afterward talked about how much joy and appreciation they felt. From then on, Greta had very happy birthdays. Greta utilized the wisdom of the Audience Member who is able to step back and view, the genius of the Score Composer who feels that something wonderful is possible, and the tactics of the Critic who motivates change. She drew upon the Stage Manager part of all her friends. People love to give, so help them out. Pave the way for others to give to you.

Guarantees To Success
- Learn the other's language.
- Be playful.
- Ask the other about what she or he needs.
- Respond graciously.
- Attend to your own needs.
- Know your essential purpose.
- Practice gratitude daily.

■ ■ ■

Each Creative Personality Type reminds you of one of life's precious gifts. The Actor reminds you to express your truest self. The Dancer reminds you to move with life's many feelings. The Critic reminds you to make life into something wonderful with your own will. The Score Composer reminds you to turn to Spirit for heart-received inspiration. The Set Designer reminds you to live practically. The Stage Manager reminds you that serving others is a pleasurable opportunity. The Playwright reminds you to constructively choose the life stories you write and live. The Director reminds you that you are not alone. The Lighting Designer reminds you to look at the good that is everywhere. The Sound Designer reminds you to create peace within. The Promoter reminds you to be enthusiastic. The Audience Member reminds you to honor others. You have access to each of the Creative Personality Types. This system was not developed so that you can classify others. It is an invitation for you to 1) appreciate all others and 2) increase your choices in responding to others, spirit, and yourself.

Creative Intimacy is a special theater production presented in a glimmering theater under stars in a forest. Tickets are free every day and never sell out. Creative Intimacy is a process in which you realize that every day has the potential for newness, joy, and celebration. Utilize your own imagination, your gifts, your talents, and co-create the play of life into all you want it to be. Set the stage with a bed of rose petals, offer the words of honey nectar, listen with the ears of enthusiasm, and carry the glimmering sword of choice. Walk hand in hand with your lover and beloved on the path of an awakening life. Choose to be creative in love, and love will be your home.

Products Created by Dr. Laurie Moore

Home is in the Heart and Communication is in the Psyche
(Meditation audiocassette tape.) $15

Co-Creating with Life and Setting Clear Intentions
(Meditation audiocassette tape.) $15

Creative Intimacy Workbook $20

■ ■ ■

Add $5 additional per order for shipping and handling (S&H).

California residents add applicable tax.

Send a list of desired items with check or money order including S&H to:

Dr. Laurie Moore

P O Box 40

Santa Cruz, CA 95063-0040

Toll Free: 1-877-291-5753

http://www.DrLaurieMoore.com